D0989933

Childhood Education

Childhood Education

Maria Montessori

Translated by
A. M. Joosten
Director, Indian Montessori Training Courses
Director, Montessori Training Center of Minnesota

Henry Regnery Company•Chicago

Library of Congress Cataloging in Publication Data

Montessori, Maria, 1870-1952.
  Childhood Education.

  Translation of Formazione dell'uomo.
  Includes bibliographical references.
  1. Education of children.   I.   Title.
LB775.M7513   1974   372.1'3   73-20433

First published in Italy under the title *Formazione dell'Uomo* by Garzanti Editore.
Published in India under the title *The Formation of Man*.
Text copyright © 1949 Mario M. Montessori, heir of Dr. Maria Montessori.
Translation copyright © 1955 A. M. Joosten.
First published in the United States 1974 by Henry Regnery Company
114 West Illinois Street, Chicago, Illinois 60610.
All rights reserved.
Manufactured in the United States of America
International Standard Book Number: 0-8092-9102-9
Library of Congress Catalog Card Number: 73-20433

Contents

Part I

Prejudices and Nebulae

1

Introduction

Contradictions

Almost half a century has gone by since we started our work. The first "Children's House" was inaugurated in 1907, and almost immediately thereafter our ideas and endeavors for child education spread all over the world. The upheavals caused by two European and world wars during the intervening years have not destroyed this educational movement, which has taken root in many countries.

With the passage of time we have become even more convinced of the importance of child education, and we wish to infuse new life into our endeavor so that it may become an effective means for the reconstruction of modern society, sadly disfigured by the ravages of these worst of all wars in history.

I feel as if I were addressing a strong family that must continue along the road we have opened up and

3

that, young and vigorous though it be, has great need of faith and hope.

I should like to give in these pages a guide for the orientation of our work. Why are there so many difficulties, so many contradictions, so much uncertainty with regard to what are commonly called "Montessori Schools" and the "Montessori Method"? Yet, in spite of this confusion and these difficulties, our schools continue to progress and expand even in the most distant lands. They can be found in the Hawaiian Islands, in Honolulu, in Greenland, and in India, among the peoples of Nigeria and of Ceylon—indeed, among all races and in all parts of the world.

Can it be that these schools, conducted by African and Indian people in backward rural areas, or for that matter, in the most civilized nations, are all perfect? Experts say that there is not so much as one good school among them; yet all agree that the Montessori Method is more widely spread than any other modern method of education. How is one to explain its popularity if many of the schools using our name fall so short of perfection? How is one to explain the fact that many nations have changed their educational laws in order not to obstruct the application of the Montessori Method? How did it spread so far afield, without any publicity campaign, when there are only a few regular reviews or organized societies working in harmony with an organic superstructure? It lacked all these aids, yet it spread like a transforming leaven, like a seed propagated by the wind!

Here is another apparent contradiction. The

Method seems egoistic; it wishes to go its own way and not to mix with any other; and yet, no other method takes every possible opportunity of inculcating world union and world peace as does this one.

All this is contradictory—even mysterious!

Today there are many important currents and personalities in the field of education. There is the New Education Fellowship, which wishes to promote harmony between and collaboration with the Montessori Method and the other new methods that continue to crop up. Everywhere this decisive step is looked for: to establish an agreement between the efforts of those who in different ways are attempting to educate the child. There is a widespread tendency to break through the isolation of our method, to make students and scientists appreciate it, and, above all, to improve and extend the training of Montessori teachers. I know that many who have dedicated their lives to this Method now face this problem of cooperation.

Another strange fact about this Method is that though originally worked out for preprimary education, it has now infiltrated into the primary and secondary stages—even into the university.

In Holland there are five Montessori lycea, the results of which have been so satisfactory that the Dutch government has not only granted them subsidies but has given them the same recognition and independence as the other recognized lycea. In Paris I saw a private Montessori Lyceum where the students were more independent in character and less scared of examinations than in other French lycea; while in

India many people have come to the conclusion that Montessori universities are a necessity.

In the opposite direction, the Montessori Method also has developed and has been applied to children under three years of age. In Ceylon two-year-old children are being admitted to our schools, while parents request admission for those of one and a half years. In England many crèches follow our Method, and in New York also Montessori crèches have been founded.[1]

What exactly, then, is this Method that begins with newborn babies and extends to undergraduates? Other methods have not so wide a function.

For example, the Froebel Method deals with children below school age only; that inspired by Pestalozzi is confined to the primary school; while the methods of Herbart deal mostly with primary and secondary education. Among the modern methods we find that of Decroly mostly in primary schools, the Dalton Plan in secondary schools, etc. Traditional methods have certainly been changed, but the teacher of one particular stage cannot teach other grades. No secondary school-teacher worries about the methods employed in pre-primary schools, still less about those employed in crèches. Each stage is clearly defined and the methods, which nowadays are constantly on the increase, are always limited to schools of one or the other of these well-defined categories.

---

[1] In Rome a training institution was founded after the last war where "assistants of infancy" are trained to assist at childbirth and during the first few years of life, according to the principles evolved by Dr. Montessori from her psychological observations of this most vital phase of development. *See* Maria Montessori: *The Absorbent Mind*—Trans.

To think of lycea using the Froebel Method would be clearly nonsensical. To advocate nursery school methods in the university would be equally so.

Why then is the application of the Montessori Method to all stages of education a matter of serious discussion? What does it mean? What is the Montessori Method thought to be?

Constant comparisons and analogies are also being made. The English nursery schools, for instance, are being compared to Montessori Schools. The toys used and the treatment of children in the former are being compared to the objects employed and the procedure adopted in the latter, in order to establish some sort of compromise between the two and amalgamate them. In the United States many parallel features have been pointed out between the Froebelian Kindergarten and the Children's Houses. While comparing the gifts of Froebel and our apparatus, it has been pointed out that both are efficient, and their conjoint use is advocated. There are only a few conflicting points, e.g., the question of fairy tales, the play with sand, the exact use of the apparatus, and certain other details about which much discussion is still going on. Also in primary schools, the methods of teaching reading, writing, and arithmetic are still being discussed. There is much controversy over our insistence on offering geometry and other advanced subjects at this early stage. Different opinions are also held regarding the teaching in secondary schools. There are those who think we do not lay sufficient stress on games and certain activities that give a modern character to teaching methods by introducing mechanical and manual crafts. Much importance is attached to those questions, since naturally the program of secondary Montessori schools has to conform with that of standard secondary schools, otherwise the students would fail to gain admission to the university.

In short, we find ourselves in a maze.

What is the Montessori Method?

One would like to know in a few clear words what this Montessori Method really is.

If we were to eliminate not only the name "method" but also its common conception, things would become much clearer. We must consider the human personality and not a method of education. For the word "method" we should substitute something like this: "Help given in order that the human personality may achieve its independence," or "means offered to deliver the human personality from the oppression of age-old prejudices regarding education." The defense of the child, the scientific recognition of his nature, and the social proclamation of his rights must replace the piecemeal ways of conceiving education.

The "human personality" belongs to all human beings. Europeans, Indians, and Chinese, etc., are all men. If, therefore, certain vital conditions are found to be a help to the human personality, these concern and affect the inhabitants of all nations.

And what is this "human personality"? Where does it begin? When does a man become a human being? This might be difficult to ascertain. According to the Old Testament man was created as an adult; in the New Testament, it is the Infant Jesus who appears. The human personality is essentially one during the successive stages of its development. Yet, whatever human being we consider and at whatever age—whether children in the primary school, adolescents, youths, or adults—all start by being children, all then grow from childhood to adulthood without changing the unity of their persons. If the human personality is one at all stages of its development, we must conceive of a principle of education that has regard to all stages. In our most recent courses, in fact, we call the child "man."

Man, the Unknown

Man, appearing in this world in the form of a child, develops rapidly by a veritable miracle of creation. The newborn possesses neither the language nor any other characteristics that reflect the customs of his kind. He has neither intelligence, memory, nor will—not even the power of moving about or keeping himself upright. Yet, this newborn realizes a real psychic creation. At two years of age he speaks, walks, recognizes people and objects in his environment, and at five, he acquires sufficient psychic development to be admitted to a school and start his formal education.

Nowadays, the scientific world is greatly interested in the psychology of the child during the first two years of life. For thousands and thousands of years, mankind had passed the child by, unimpressed by this miracle of nature—for the formation of the intelligence of a human personality is certainly a miracle. How is it formed? By means of what processes and in obedience to what laws?

If the whole universe is governed by fixed laws, is it possible that the human mind be formed haphazardly, i.e., without any law at all?

Everything in the course of development passes through a complex process of evolution. Man, too, who at five years of age has become an intelligent being, must have gone through a constructive evolution.

This field, we must admit, has hitherto been unexplored. There is a vacuum in our present scientific knowledge, an unexplored territory, an unknown factor—and this void concerns the process of the formation of the personality.

The persistence of such ignorance at the level of civilization to which we have attained must have mysterious causes. Something has remained buried in the subconscious, and an encrustation of prejudices, difficult to break through, has formed over it. In order to start the scientific exploration of this immense and obscure field of the human spirit, we must overcome powerful obstacles. We only know that in the human psyche there exists an enigma, not yet touched upon by our interest, just as a short time ago we only knew there was an immense area of ice at the South Pole. The Antarctic exploration was then undertaken and a whole continent, full of marvels and wealth, emerged on the horizon of our mind. Its wonders, its warm-water lakes, its large living beings, whose very existence had been unsuspected, then stood revealed. But to reach these realities what obstacles had to be overcome, what massive barriers of ice had to be broken through, and what a freezing climate, so different from ours, had to be braved! The same applies to that pole of human life—early childhood.

It appears to the adult that he comes from an unknown source. He judges the various aspects of his life as he finds them. His efforts to lead human beings in their successive stages—as children, adolescents, youths, etc.—are therefore empirical and superficial. As a clumsy cultivator, he judges appearances and effects without worrying about the causes that produce them. Rightly, Froebel calls the school for children of four or five years of age "kindergarten" (garden of children). It is what all schools could be called—especially the better types where a serious effort is made to benefit the children and promote their happiness. All could be called "gardens" to distinguish them from those schools where only a cruel tyranny reigns. In fact, in the more modern and better schools, those that correspond to Froebel's ideals, the educators behave as do good gardeners and cultivators towards their plants.

Behind the good cultivator, however, stands the scientist who scrutinizes the secrets of nature. His experiments enable him to acquire profound knowledge, which helps not only to a better understanding of the plants, but which can be used to transform them. The modern cultivator, who multiplies the varieties of flowers and fruits, who reclaims forests, who, we may say, changes the face of the earth, gathers his technical principles from science, not from customary practices. Thus, those marvelous flowers with their varied beauty, those double carnations with all their different hues, those superb orchids, those giant roses so fragrant and without thorns, the many fruits, and all the marvels that have changed the face of the earth are the outcome of man's scientific study of plant life. It was science that offered a new technique. It was the scientist who gave the impetus to the construction of a real "supranature" fantastically more rich and beautiful than what we now call "wild nature."

The Study of Man

If science began to study man, it would not only succeed in offering new techniques for the education of children and the young, it would further lead to a profound understanding of many human and social phenomena that are still enveloped in obscurity.

The basis of the reform of education and society, which is a necessity of our times, must be built upon the scientific study of Man, the Unknown.

As we mentioned, however, there is a great obstacle to the scientific study of man. This obstacle is formed by the prejudices accumulated during thousands of years that have become as solid, as majestic, and almost as inaccessible as glaciers. A courageous exploration is therefore needed, a struggle against adverse elements for which the ordinary weapons of science, i.e., observation and experiment, do not suffice.

This study of the spirit of man, of psychology, has grown into an intellectual movement that has spread since the beginning of our century. The discovery of the subconscious has been especially fruitful, first in making contact with adults suffering from mental diseases, and then extending to adults considered normal. More recently child psychology has begun to interest students of this science. The conclusion reached, as a result of these studies, was that almost all men now living have some imperfection in their mental makeup, and statistics irrefutably reveal an ever growing number of lunatics and psychopathological criminals. They also show that the number of "problem children" is on the increase and stress the growing phenomenon of juvenile delinquency, which is thought-provoking on account of the harm it does to humanity. Evidently the social conditions produced by our civilization create obstacles for the normal development of man.

Our civilization has not yet devised means of defense for the spirit similar to those devised for the body through physical hygiene. While nowadays we control and utilize the material wealth of the earth and its energies, no consideration has yet been given to that supreme energy represented by the human intellect. While the hidden potentialities of nature have been explored and exploited to their very utmost, the abyss of man's subconscious has not yet been scanned. Man, as a spiritual being, has been left to the mercy of outer circumstances and is on the way to becoming a destroyer of his own constructions.

It is, therefore, possible to conceive a universal movement for human reconstruction that follows a single path. Its sole aim is to help man to preserve his balance, his psychic health, and build up a secure orientation in the present conditions of our outer world. This movement is not limited to any one nation nor to any particular political trend because it aims at the simple realization of human values, and that is what is of primary interest over and above all political or national differences.

The conceptions of the old schools, where teaching continues in the same way as in times profoundly different from ours, are clearly inadequate in view of the aims of the new movement we have outlined above.

Education now becomes a social and human endeavor of interest to all. It must be based on psychology in order to safeguard the individuality of the child. It must furthermore be oriented towards a clear understanding of our civilization so that the personality defended against the disorder of circumstances may become a human being conscious of his real position in history. Evidently a syllabus or curriculum arbitrarily drawn up cannot ensure the culture we need today. There is need of a syllabus that can give an understanding of the conditions of man in modern society with a cosmic vision of history and the evolution of human life. What purpose would education serve in our days unless it helped man to a knowledge of the environment to which he has to adapt himself!

Finally, the problems of education must be solved on the basis of the laws of the cosmic order. These laws reach from the eternal laws governing the psychic construction of human life to the changing laws that lead society along the road of evolution on earth.

Respect for these cosmic laws is fundamental. Only when we hold to these as basic can we judge and modify the multitude of human laws that deal with the passing moments of external social construction.

Our Social Present

It is a commonplace to assert that there exists a lack of balance between the miraculous progress of our environment and the arrest of development suffered by man. Everyone knows that man meets with great difficulties in his adaptation to his environment and that he suffers and deteriorates in the process. We might compare the forces of outer progress to those of a powerful nation that invades and crushes a weaker one, and, as always happens in barbaric wars, the vanquished is enslaved.

Today mankind is vanquished and enslaved by its own environment because it has remained weak in comparison with that environment.

This slavery is growing rapidly and is now assuming forms never experienced in the past struggles between powerful, victorious peoples, and weak, vanquished ones. Never before did human helplessness reach that extreme point witnessed in our days.

Do we not see that nothing is any longer secure? Money kept in banks may in various ways be suddenly and irretrievably lost to its owner, and should an attempt be made to safeguard it by hiding it in secret places, as was done in the Middle Ages, it may lose its value and be withdrawn from circulation. The money of one country cannot be taken into another. Even a wealthy person cannot now go to live in the country of his choice, for he may not carry money or jewelry across the border. There is the risk of visitation at frontier posts where people are undressed and searched as if their property had been stolen. One can travel only with passports, which are now a nuisance instead of a protection as they were originally intended to be. Even in one's own country, one is obliged, especially during a war, to carry about on one's person an identity card containing one's photograph and fingerprints—a thing not imposed even on criminals in former days. It has happened to us to be allowed to buy only what is strictly necessary for life and to have to depend on coupons distributed at regular intervals to buy even bread. Such a thing was unheard of before, except in the case of mendicants.

Nowadays nobody's life is safe. An absurd war may be declared in which all men—young and old, women and children—are in mortal danger. Civilians are bombed, and people have to take refuge in underground shelters, just as primitive men took refuge in caves to defend themselves against wild beasts. The supply of food may be cut off and millions may die of famine and plague. Do we not see men in rags or even naked, freezing to death, families separated and torn apart, children abandoned and roaming about in wild hordes?

This we see, not only among those vanquished in war, but everywhere. Humanity itself is vanquished and enslaved—but why enslaved? Because all—victors and vanquished—all men are slaves, insecure, frightened, suspicious, and hostile, compelled to defend themselves by means of spying and brigandage, using and fostering immorality as a means of defense. Cheating and robbing appear in a changed light and are considered means of survival where restrictions reach an absurd level. Vileness, prostitution, and violence become quite common modes of living. Spiritual and intellectual values that once honored human society lose their bearings. Study becomes an arid, weary pursuit without any uplifting influence. It is undertaken only as a means to get a job, which in its turn is uncertain and insecure.

It is strikingly impressive that humanity, despite its nameless slavery, forms a kind of stereotyped chorus crying out that it is free and independent. These miserable and degraded people proclaim their own sovereignty. What do these unfortunates look for? They seek as their greatest good what they call *democracy*, i.e., that the people may give their opinion as to how they are to be ruled—that they may cast their votes at elections. What irony! To choose one's rulers! But those who rule cannot free anybody from the chains that bind all, that render all activity and initiative futile, and that render them helpless to save themselves.

The master of all is a mysterious entity. The tyrant is all powerful, like a god. It is the environment that swallows up and crushes the man.

The other day a young baker, who worked in a big mechanized bakery, had his hands caught between the wheels that then trapped his whole body and reduced it to pulp. Is not that a symbol of the conditions in which mankind languishes, unconsciously, a victim of its fate? This environment can be compared to that colossal engine that can produce fabulous quantities of food, and the workman it entrapped represents our unwary and imprudent humanity that is grabbed and crushed by what should give it abundance. Here we see one aspect of the lack of balance between man and his environment from which humanity must deliver itself by strengthening its own resources, developing its own values, healing its own madness, and becoming conscious of its own power.

Man must gather together all his values and energies; he must develop them and prepare himself for his liberation. This is not the time to fight each other, to try to subdue each other. We must consider man alone and strive to raise him up, to strip him of the useless bonds he creates for himself that push him downwards into the abyss of lunacy. The real enemy is man's impotence against his own products; it is the arrest of the development of humanity itself. To vanquish this enemy, man has only to react to and behave in a different manner towards the environment, which in itself is a source of wealth and happiness. A universal revolution is what we need. This revolution requires only that man should raise his values and become the master, instead of the victim, of the environment he himself has created.

The Task of New Education

It may seem that we have drifted rather far from our original subject—education. This digression, however, must open up the new road, along which we have to go now. In the same way in which we help the patients in a hospital recover their health and continue to live, so we must now help humanity to save itself. We must be nurses in a hospital as vast as the world itself.

We must realize that the problem in question is not confined to schools as they are conceived today and that it does not concern methods of education more or less practical, more or less philosophical.

Either education contributes to a movement of universal liberation by showing the way to defend and raise humanity, or it becomes like an organ that has shriveled up by not being used during the evolution of the organism.

We already mentioned that there is in our day a totally new scientific movement that presents results, at present disconnected—spread here and there—but certainly tending to unify themselves in the near future.

This movement, however, is not really part of education; it belongs rather to the field of psychology. Even in psychology it did not emerge from a pedagogical impulse—to know man in order to educate him—but was rather stimulated by the desire to assuage the sufferings and abnormalities of mankind—especially of adults. This new psychology, therefore, was born in the field of medicine, not in that of education. This psychology of diseased humanity turned its attention also to children who seemed agitated and unhappy, and it discovered that their vital energies were repressed and deviated from the path of normality.

In any case, this is the scientific movement that is taking shape, and it aims at building up some barrier against the ever spreading evil and at prescribing some remedy for the confused and disoriented soul of man. Education must attach itself to this movement.

Believe me, the attempts of so-called modern education, which simply tries to deliver the child from presumed repression, are not on the right path. To let the pupils do what they like, to amuse them with light occupations, to lead them back to an almost wild state, does not solve the problem. The question is not to deliver man from some bonds, but *to reconstruct*, and reconstruction requires the elaboration of a "science of the human spirit." It is a patient work, an endeavor based on research, to which thousands of people dedicated to this aim must contribute.

Whoever works for this ideal must be actuated by a great ideal, much greater than those political ideals that have promoted social improvements, that concern only the material life of some groups of men oppressed by injustice or misery. This ideal is universal in its scope. It aims at the deliverance of the whole of humanity. Much patient work, I repeat, is needed along this road towards the freedom and "valorization" of mankind.

Look at what happens in the field of other sciences! How many people work in closed laboratories, observing cells under the microscope, discovering the miracles of life! How many pass their lives in chemistry laboratories, testing reactions, discovering the secrets of matter! How many are laboring to isolate cosmic energies in order to capture and utilize them! It is these innumerable patient and sincere workers who have advanced civilization.

Something similar, therefore, has to be done for man himself. The ideal, the proposed aim, however, must be common to all. Its realization must lead to what has been said in regard to man in the Scriptures: *"Specie tua et pulchritudine tua intende, prospere procede et regna!"* We might paraphrase it thus: "Understand thyself and thy beauty, proceed prosperously in thine environment, rich and full of miracles, and reign over it!"

Now you may say: "Yes, all this is very beautiful and fascinating, but do you not see how, in the meantime, everywhere around us children grow up, young boys become full-grown men? We cannot wait for any scientific elaboration because, meanwhile, mankind will be destroyed."

I would answer: "It is not necessary that the whole work of research be accomplished. It is enough that the idea be understood and that the work be taken in hand following its indications."

Meanwhile, one thing is clear: Pedagogy must not be guided, as in the past, by the ideas that some philosophers and philanthropists formed of it, by some individuals inspired by piety, sympathy, or charity. Pedagogy must follow the guidance of psychology, by that psychology that applied to education should at once be given a distinct name—psychopedagogy.

Many discoveries have yet to be made in this field. There is no doubt that the liberation of man will give stupendous revelations if he is still repressed and unknown.

Education must proceed along the path lit up by these revelations, just as common medicine is based on the *vis medicatrix naturae*, on the curative forces already existing in nature, and hygiene is based on the natural functions of the body.

To help life—this is the first and fundamental principle.

Who, then, can reveal the natural ways along which the psychic development of man proceeds but the child himself, once he is placed in conditions permitting him to do so?

Our first teacher, therefore, will be the child himself, or rather the vital urge with the cosmic laws that lead him unconsciously. Not what we call the child's

will, but the mysterious will that directs his formation—
this must be our guide.

I may affirm that the revelations of the child are
not at all so difficult to obtain: the real difficulty lies
in the adult's old prejudices concerning him. It lies in
the total lack of understanding and in the veil that
an arbitrary form of education, based only on human
reasoning and still more on the unconscious egoism
of man and his pride as a dominator, have been
weaving, so that the values of wise nature are hidden.

Our contribution—however small and still incomplete, however insignificant in the opinion of those
working in the field of scientific psychology—will serve
precisely to illustrate this enormous obstacle of prejudices that are capable of cancelling and destroying
the contributions of our isolated experience. We would
already have conferred a benefit of general importance
were we only to succeed in proving the existence of
these prejudices.

Part II

Prejudices in Science and Education

1

The Revelation of the Natural Order in Children and Its Obstacles

Revelations and Obstacles

LET us keep well in mind how our study came into being. About forty years ago a group of four-year-old children revealed an unexpected phenomenon that caused great amazement. This phenomenon was called "the explosion into writing." Some children spontaneously started to write, and their example was at once followed by a great number of their companions. There was a real explosion of activity and enthusiasm. Those small children carried the letters of the alphabet in a kind of triumphal procession with shouts of joy. They continued writing without any sign of fatigue or boredom. They covered the floor and walls with their unrestrainable writing. Their progress was really marvelous. Soon afterwards, they began to read by themselves all types of writing—cursive script, print, small and capital letters, and even special artistic and Gothic lettering.

Now let us examine this first revelation for a while. It was evidently a revelation of a psychological nature and sufficiently powerful to attract the attention of the world at the time. It was a kind of miracle.

Yet what was the reaction, especially of the scientists of the day?

The marvelous writing was not attributed to a psychological fact but to a "method of education."

Writing and nature could not be associated. Generally, writing is the result of a painful and disagreeable preparation in school. It evokes the memory of dry effort, of pains suffered, and punishment inflicted. It reminds us of a torment gone through by all who are not illiterate. The method that had succeeded in obtaining such brilliant results at such a precocious age must, therefore, have been really marvelous. Curiosity arose concerning this method of education that proved to have found at last a means to overcome so quickly illiteracy, which had lingered on more or less even among civilized nations.

When some university professors from the United States came to me to study this method personally, I could not show any other apparatus than the cut-out letters of the alphabet. These letters were objects that could be handled and put here and there, and they were rather large in size.

Some of these professors were offended and felt that I was making fun of them. In lofty scientific circles, it was being said that all this was not serious. To speak of miracles was a mystification. When it became known later on that instead of books we used "objects" that could be bought and sold, there was a kind of fear to be mixed up with some commercial enterprise. A kind of amour propre withheld the attention of the great from these manifestations that, nonetheless, were connected with an unknown factor of a psychological nature. Thus an obstacle was put in its way—*an insurmountable barrier was raised between that illuminating experience and those very people who, by virtue of their culture, should have been able to interpret and utilize it.*

Let us pass on to other forms of prejudice.

Those small children, who wrote on and on without ever tiring, were a reality that hundreds and thousands of people could see for themselves. Many people had to convince themselves that the letters of the alphabet were simply placed in the environment, each one separate, and that no teacher made an effort to teach the children to write. The children evidently achieved this on their own. Some people consequently began to think that the whole secret lay in the idea of isolating the letters of the alphabet and employing them as moveable objects. What a simple discovery of genius! "Why," many of them regretfully wondered, "why did I not think of it myself?" But someone ventured, "This is not a discovery at all. Already in ancient times Quintilian used such a kind of moveable alphabet." Had I wished, therefore, to pose as an inventor and a genius I would have been shown up.

It is curious, however, to notice such a widely spread mental inertia, which stops short before an external object without being able, one might say, to go further and consider some new psychological fact with regard to the child. This concerns a real mental barrier common to all, both cultured and uncultured.

Yet it would have been so simple to reflect that if in history the moveable alphabet of Quintilian is still remembered, the reactions provoked by it ought equally to have been remembered. Were there processions of enthusiastic people, mad with joy, who strode through the streets of Rome carrying banners with the letters of the alphabet on them? Did the people who came in contact with its magic learn by themselves, and did they cover the roads and the walls of the houses with written words? Did all learn to read by themselves, and not only Roman script, but Greek as well? History would certainly have recorded such impressive happenings, but evidently nothing of the kind did happen, for only the moveable letters are remembered. The magic does not lie in them, but in the psychology of the child. At the time, nobody would admit this. The prejudice that forbids us to "believe the extraordinary," the fear of being thought credulous, which is felt by those who wish to uphold their dignity and cultural superiority, is common to all. It is one of the obstacles that hides what is "new" and renders a discovery useless.

A discovery, to be real, must contain something new. This element of novelty is an open door to those who have the courage to go through. It is a door that gives access to hitherto unexplored fields. It is therefore a fantastic, marvelous door, which ought to strike the imagination. The people of superior culture are really those who ought logically to become the explorers of these fields. A mental and emotional barrier, however, stands in the way of these serious-minded persons, who have lost all relish for the "fairy tales" of nature. It is extremely rare to find an exception to this rule.

Already the famous banquet in the Gospel expressed this eternal fact in symbolic form by implying that a certain degree of simplicity and "poverty" is needed to enter the new realm.

As an example of such barriers we may quote the fate suffered by C. F. Wolff, who was the first to discover the constructive process leading from a germinal cell to the embryo and ultimately to the hatched chick. His discoveries met with the concerted opposition of all other scientists of his day who were all involved in the dispute between animalculists and ovulists. They were prejudiced by philosophical theories and would not admit the factual material presented by this young discoverer in his *Theoria Generationis*. He had to leave his country and died in exile. Only fifty years later, when another scientist, K. E. von Baer, repeated Wolff's investigations full credit was given to him and his predecessor, and then there was born the new science of embryology.

But let it be noted that this recognition was given to a discovery relating to the embryo. Too many prejudices and too many vested interests are accumulated where children are concerned. I mean above all the interest created in protecting children from "mental effort," "precocious intellectual activity," etc. In everybody's eyes children are empty beings only suited for play, sleep, and the pastime of fantastic tales. Serious mental work done by such young children seems sacrilegious, all the more so after the insistent publications of Charlotte Bühler, the wife of the well-known Viennese psychologist Karl Bühler and herself an authoritative exponent of experimental psychology. Charlotte Bühler reached the conclusion that the mental faculties of children under five years of age are impermeable to any form of culture. Thus, in the name of science, a kind of tombstone was placed over our experiments.

The phenomena observed by us among young children were attributed exclusively to a "method of education" that besides was uncertain and disputable. Then the battle of the critics began. The discussion concerned above all the question that the mental life of children ought not to be immolated in favor of useless results because a little later on, after six years of age, all can learn to read and to write, and everybody knows at the cost of what effort and sacrifice. We must spare the early years of childhood the painful labor of intellectual study. Claparède, a great authority on pedagogical matters, described, on behalf of the New Education Fellowship, all the damage done to pupils by study in schools. His argument was somewhat as follows: "It is true that our civilization requires study as a necessity, but if it harms the child we must try to minimize this harm!" The new schools, therefore, tried to eliminate and have gradually withdrawn from the curricula many subjects not considered necessary, e.g., geometry, grammar, and a great deal of mathematics, and have substituted games and open-air life instead.

Alas, the world of official education too put our work aside! The teachers, moreover, who learned from us at the beginning were mostly people dedicated to education in the Froebel Kindergarten, and thus "gifts" of Froebel were mixed up with our scientific apparatus for mental development, and the conclusion reached was that both contained some good parts, but that the alphabet, writing, and mathematics should not be introduced into schools for very young children.

Then the teachers of primary schools tried the experiment with the alphabet, but they could arouse no enthusiasm or "explosion" either. The only thing that happened was that a freer form of study slipped into the ordinary schools and that individual occupations and objects were given.

The "miracle" was officially relegated to oblivion. It did not succeed in attracting the interest of modern psychology. It was thus left to me to investigate the secrets of child psychology that this experiment revealed. Nobody better than I could "isolate" these real facts from any educational influence capable of evoking them. It was clear to me that some "energy" peculiar to children at that age had become manifest and consequently existed.

Even if our experience had been limited to this first group of children, this phenomenon would have been a discovery of powers of the child psyche that hitherto had been hidden.

Did it not seem a miracle, or perhaps better, a queer occurrence, when Galvani saw dead and skinned frogs, which had been tied to a window railing, move their legs? If he had thought that he was witnessing a "miracle of resurrection" or an optical illusion, his intelligence would never have persisted in questioning its cause nor would he ever have obeyed its urge to investigate the matter. "If dead frogs move, there must be an energy that makes them do so," he reasoned—

and thus electricity was discovered. The development of electricity and its applications went a long distance beyond this revealing phenomenon.

If somebody had wanted to repeat the experiment literally in order to prove it, the miracle might never have been obtained and it would have been thought that the whole thing had been an illusion not worthy of entering into the field of science.

Previous Revelations

Our children were not the first to reveal psychic energies that generally remain hidden. They were, however, the youngest to do so. Previously, similar revelations had been given by children over seven years of age. The history of pedagogy, in fact, gives an account of the "miracles" of the school run by Pestalozzi at Stanz. All of a sudden his wards were enveloped, as it were, by an atmosphere of unforeseen progress. Those children did things considered beyond their age. Some made such progress in mathematics that their parents withdrew them from Pestalozzi's institution lest they should suffer from mental fatigue. Pestalozzi, in his description of their spontaneous and indefatigable work, followed by such prodigious progress, makes an eloquent confession of the fact that he had nothing to do with these marvelous phenomena. He says, "I was only an amazed onlooker."

Then the flame went out, and under the benevolent and affectionate care of Pestalozzi everything returned to normal. It is interesting to know what his admirers, and especially the Swiss, who are so proud of him, thought about it. All of them were of the opinion that the phenomenon at Stanz belonged to a period of craziness in their hero, and they rejoiced that he could come back to "serious work."

Thus pedagogy had its triumph by burying a revelation of a psychological nature.

Tolstoy describes something similar about the peasant children he educated with such enthusiasm and affection in the school at Yasnaja Poliana. Suddenly these children began to read the Bible passionately. They came to school in the morning earlier than usual to read alone, without any sign of fatigue. They showed a joy they had never shown before. Then, too, Tolstoy witnessed a "return to normality."

How many similar facts, of which we know nothing, must have happened in the lives of children, but they were unperceived and so remain unrecorded in the history of pedagogy.

The Mental Form of Childhood

There is, therefore, an inner energy that of its nature tends to manifest itself, but remains buried under universal prejudices. There is a *mental form* peculiar to childhood that has never been recognized.

It was indeed a "mental form" and not only the phenomenon of explosive writing that revealed itself among my children in the first Children's House in San Lorenzo.

It happened that when very long words were dictated to them—even foreign words—they reproduced them phonetically with the moveable alphabet, having heard them only once. All those who have read my books know of these phenomena.[1] We dictated, for instance, words like *Darmstadt, Sangiaccato di Novi Bazar, Precipitevolissimevolmente.*

What fixed these complicated words in the minds of the children so that they seemed to retain them with a certainty as if they had been sculptured in their memory? The most marvelous thing was their calmness and simplicity, as if they did not make any effort. It must be remembered that they did *not write*—they had to find each letter in the different compartments of the alphabet box. One has to look for the compartment of each letter, which is not easy, then take the letter and put it beside the others already in place, so as to complete the word. This would have distracted the attention of any of us.

This astonished the technicians of ordinary education, especially because it is known how difficult dictation is in primary schools. We all know how often a good teacher must repeat every word while the child writes it, even in the case of pupils of eight years and over. The reason alleged is that the child forgets what he is writing. That is also the reason why at first only short and well-known words are given.

Let us recall here the famous anecdote of Inspector of Schools Di Donato. Once he came to see our school with a rather severe expression on his face, as a man well-armed against possible delusions. He did not wish to dictate long and difficult words, which might hide some trick. He simply dictated his own name, Di Donato, to a four-year-old child. This child evidently did not

---

[1]*See* Maria Montessori: *The Discovery of the Child.*

catch the pronunciation well and understood, "Ditonato" and began to put the third letter down as a "t." The inspector, faithful to his educational methods, immediately corrected, by repeating his name more clearly. The child was not confused. To him, evidently, it was not a matter of correction or error, but only of not hearing quite distinctly. He took the "t" and instead of putting it back in its compartment in the box, placed it aside on his table. He calmly continued to compose the name and when he came to the end, he took the discarded "t" and used it. The whole name, therefore, had been impressed upon his mind, and the interruption had not created any difficulty. From the beginning he knew that a "t" was needed to complete the word. That was what made such a great impression on the inspector, who exclaimed, "The mistake was the most eloquent proof of the truth. I confess that I did not believe in this suprising fact, but now I am convinced. I must say, it is incredible, but true!" Then without remembering to praise the child whom he had remembered to correct, he turned to me: "I congratulate you. It is really a remarkable method; we must use it in our schools." Is it not clear that for a technician of education there could be the question only of a better or worse "method"? The psychological fact remained foreign to him. The barrier of prejudice made it impossible for the educator to understand the phenomenon. On leaving, he still thought about it and remarked, "With ordinary methods not even a child of nine could have done that." The compliment was addressed to me! . . .

Yet this incident showed a fact regarding the

memory. The thought that there could be a form of memory in younger children different from that of older children could not be conceived. The younger child must have a memory feebler than that of the child five years older!

What, however, was there peculiar in the memory of the young child? Evidently the word, in all its details, was sculptured in his memory. The word, the sounds that compose it, and their correct succession remained complete in his mind—nothing could efface them. That memory was of a different nature from that of older children. It created a kind of vision in the mind, and the child reproduced this clear and fixed vision with certainty.

The Mneme

Is it then possible that there exists a memory different from that of our conscious and developed minds?

Some psychologists of our day speak of a form of unconscious memory that retains its fixed images even through generations and minutely reproduces the characteristics of the species. They have given it a distinctive name—"mneme." The mneme, with its infinite gradations, penetrates into the very facts of life and eternity. Once this has been ascertained, it is easy to recognize in the mind of the four-year-old child a phase of psychic development in which the mneme stands on the very threshold of conscious memory, almost on the point of merging with it, yet manifesting itself as the last trace of a phenomenon with very deep roots.

That last trace of the mneme came from afar. It is linked up with the creative forces of language. The mother tongue was already formed in the unconscious as the result of a process different from that followed by the conscious mind. The mother tongue is the language that is fixed in one's personality as a vital characteristic. It differs from the foreign languages one can acquire with the help of conscious memory—those are always imperfect and can be retained only by constant practice.

The moveable letters clearly represent objects that have a bearing on the sounds fixed in the child's mind, and they bring his language into the outer world in a tangible form. The interest shown in writing comes from within. A creative sensibility is still vibrating, like that destined by nature to fix the spoken language of man, and from this sensitivity arose such enthusiasm for the alphabet.

The Italian alphabet has only twenty-one letters to express the sounds of the language—yet all the innumerable words, so many that even a voluminous dictionary could not contain them all, can be composed with these twenty-one letters. This alphabet was therefore sufficient to reproduce the patrimony of words that the child had accumulated during his development. It was sufficient to release almost suddenly the explosion of this accumulated language, and the child joyfully lived this miracle.

Discipline

Let us examine another set of prejudices that formed a great obstacle to the understanding of our work.

There was the question raised with regard to "discipline," to the amazing phenomenon shown by those small children who remained orderly and quiet, though they were free to choose their occupations and were not hindered in continuing their exercises as long as they were interested in them.

They were capable of maintaining this orderly behavior even when the teacher was absent. This collective behavior, remarkable for its social harmony and the features of its character, which did not show any sign of envy or competition but led them to help each other, aroused admiration. They "loved silence" and sought it as a real source of joy.

Obedience developed through successive degrees to a high degree of perfection, reaching finally that stage where "obedience was given with joy." There was, I might say, an "anxiousness" to obey, which might remind us of that shown by members of a religious community.

No activity on the part of the teacher was needed to obtain this strange phenomenon. It was, in other words, not a direct result of education, because there were no instructions, no admonitions and neither rewards nor punishments, but everything happened spontaneously.

Yet this unusual fact had to have some cause; it had to be produced by some influence. To those who asked me for an explanation, I could at the time only reply, "It is freedom that produces it," as I had replied to queries regarding the explosion of writing by saying, "It is the moveable alphabet."

I remember how a minister of state, without

bothering much about the feature of spontaneity, once said to me, "You have solved a great problem; you have succeeded in fusing together discipline and freedom—this is not a problem that concerns the government of schools only, it concerns the government of nations."

Evidently, in this case also, it was understood by implication that I had had the power of obtaining such results. It was I who had solved a problem. The mentality of people could not conceive this other idea that the nature of childhood can offer a solution for a problem that we adults cannot solve—that from the child came the fusion of what our mind conceives only as a contrast.

The correct thing to say, in face of such facts, would have been, "Let us study these phenomena; let us work together in order to penetrate into the secrets of the human psyche." But it was impossible for all to understand that from the depths of the child's soul we can draw something new, something useful for all of us, some light that would clarify the obscure causes of human behavior.

It would be interesting to record the opinions and criticisms voiced on all sides by philosophers, pedagogists, and even by the public.

Some said, "You do not realize what you have achieved! You are not aware of the great work you have done!" Others exclaimed, "How can you be so optimistic about human nature?" as if my description of these phenomena were some imaginative tale or something I had dreamt. The real struggle, which has not stopped yet, was carried on, however, by the philosophers and many religious men who attributed to opinions of mine the facts that so many hundreds of people had witnessed. To some I was a follower of Rousseau. I, evidently, had decided to agree with him that "in man all is good, but everything is spoilt in contact with society." I was supposed to have created in my schools, as Rousseau had done in one of his books, a kind of romantic story.

All the same, while discussing with me, no clear explanation or conviction could be drawn, and a well-known person wrote in an influential paper, "Montessori is a poor philosopher!"

According to the religious, I almost went against the faith and many of them thronged around me to explain the reality of "original sin." It is easy to imagine what Calvinists or Protestants in general thought about it, convinced as they are of the innate and total evil of human nature!

Not only were the principles of the various philosophies concerning the nature of the human soul offended, but the principles of the technique of school education were equally offended. Our method was spoken of as aprioristic, as abolishing rewards and punishments, and proposing to obtain discipline without these practical aids. It was judged to be pedagogically "absurd" and in contradiction to universal practical experience, even as sacrilegious, as it is said that God rewards the good and chastises the wicked, which is for many the most real support of morals.

There was a group of English teachers who protested publicly and declared that if punishments were abolished, they would resign from teaching because they could not educate without punishments.

Punishments! I had not realized that they were an indispensable institution holding sway over the whole of child humanity. All men have grown up under this humiliation!

An inquiry regarding punishments was held by the League of Nations at Geneva, organized by the Institute Jean-Jacques Rousseau in cooperation with the New Education Fellowship. Educational institutions and private homes were asked what kind of punishments they used to educate the children. It is curious that instead of feeling offended at such an indiscreet inquiry all hastened to submit information, and some institutions seemed proud of their mode of punishing. Some, for instance, said that immediate punishment was forbidden, lest it be administered in a state of anger, but shortcomings were faithfully recorded and on the weekend, on the sabbath of repose, the dose of punishment deserved for the whole week was administered.

Some families replied, "We are not violent when the child is naughty. We send him to bed without supper."

There is, however, no doubt that violent punishment was very much in favor—slaps, insults, beatings, locking-up, terrible imaginary scares, etc. The list received by the League of Nations in our century was an exemplification of Solomon's proverb, "Spare the rod and spoil the child."

In London, I myself could buy whips sold in bundles, as they were still used by the teachers.

The necessity for these "indispensable means" of education proves that the life of childhood was not and is not democratic and that its human dignity is not respected. From the most ancient times a barrier has been raised in the heart even more than in the mind of the adult. The inner powers of the child have never been realized, neither from the intellectual nor from the moral point of view.

In my experiences the revelation of the children's unknown inner powers eliminated punishments; yet all this, appearing suddenly on account of a fortunate set of circumstances and as an unexpected, yet immediate, revelation, remained incomprehensible to others and caused scandal.

Let me explain by means of an illustration. When something is shown to a dog by pointing the index finger at it with the intention that the dog should go and fetch the object indicated, it will stare fixedly at the finger instead of at the object. It would in the end be more likely that he would snap at the finger instead of going towards the object pointed out to him. The barrier of prejudices in the adult acts in the same way. People looked at me as if I were such an outstretched finger, and in the end snapped at me, too.

It was impossible for them to accept simply the evidence of the facts. These facts, in their opinion, had to be somebody's achievement. Somebody had either to produce them or imagine them.

That is why we speak of a blind spot in the heart of man, notwithstanding his capacity to understand so much. This blind spot is similar to that in the retina of the eye, which, nevertheless, is the organ by which all things are seen. The moral vision of the child falls upon the "blind spot" of the human heart and there it strikes a barrier of ice.

We have also spoken of the "blank page" in the history of mankind—that is the page that has never been written—the page referring to the child.

In the colossal and innumerable volumes written on the history of man the child never appears. Never is he taken into account in politics, in social construction, in war, or in reconstruction. The adult speaks as if he, the adult, alone existed. The child belongs to one's private life—he is something claiming duties and sacrifices from the adult and deserves punishment whenever he disturbs him. When the adult dreams of an earthly paradise in a future world, he sees only Adam and Eve and the serpent; in this paradise there is no child.

Our social mentality has not yet grasped the idea that we can receive help from the child, that the child can give us a light and a lesson, a new vision and a solution for inextricable problems. Even psychologists do not see in him an open door through which they may enter the subconscious. Even they still try to discover and decipher him through the ills of the adult only.

Order and Goodness

To return to the subject of moral barriers, it was really quite simple to understand the phenomenon of those children's spontaneous discipline and their social behavior, which was so marvelously delicate, sure, and perfect.

When we gaze at the stars twinkling in the sky, ever faithfully following their orbit, so steadfast in their position, do we think, "Oh! how good the stars are?" No, we only say, "The stars obey the laws that govern the universe," and we say, "How marvelous is the order of creation!"

A *form of order* in nature also appears in the behavior of children.

Order does not necessarily mean goodness. This order does not at all prove that man "is born good," or that he is born evil. It proves only that nature, in its process of constructing man, follows an established order.

Order is not goodness, but perhaps it is an indispensable way to attain it.

Also our outer social organization needs order as its foundation. The social laws regulating the conduct of citizens and the police force that controls them are of basic necessity in a social structure. Yet government embodying these institutions can be bad, unjust, and cruel. Even war, which is the least good and most inhuman feature of social life, is based on discipline and obedience on the part of the soldiers. The goodness of a government and the discipline it maintains are two distinct things. Similarly, in schools there can be no education unless discipline is first obtained—yet there can be good and bad forms of education.

Here among these children, order came from mysterious, hidden, inner directives, which can manifest themselves only if the freedom permitting them to be heeded is given. In order to give this type of freedom, it was precisely necessary that nobody interfere to obstruct the constructive, spontaneous activity of the children in an environment prepared so that their need for development could find satisfaction.

Before we can reach the point where we are "good" we must first enter into the "order of the laws of nature." Then from this level we can raise ourselves and ascend to a "supernature" where the cooperation of consciousness is necessary.

Regarding evil and badness, we must also distinguish "disorder" from a descent to a lower moral plane. To be disorderly regarding the natural laws that rule the normal development of the child does not necessarily mean to be "bad." The English, in fact, use different terms to indicate the "badness" of children and that of adults. They call the former "naughtiness" and the latter "wickedness" or "badness."

We can now state with certainty that the naughtiness of young children represents a disorder regarding the natural laws of psychic life in the course of construction. It is not badness but it does compromise the future normality of the psychic functioning of the individual.

Health and Deviations

If instead of normality we say "health" when referring to the psychical health of children during growth, everything becomes clearer, as it makes us think of similar facts in the functioning of the body. We say that a body is healthy when all its organs function normally. That criterion applies to all men, whether they be strong or weak, or whatever their physical temperament may be. If, however, some organ

does not function well, we face "functional diseases."
These have nothing to do with lesions, with organic
diseases. They are the result of abnormal functioning.
Such functional diseases can be corrected with the help
of hygienic treatment, exercises, and the like. Let us
carry over this set of conceptions into the psychic field.
There, too, there are functions that can be disturbed.
They do not at all depend on racial characteristics or on
a particular individual type or on an ego predestined
to great or miserable achievements in life. The genius,
as well as the ordinary individual, must have certain
functions normally established—he must be psychically
healthy.

Now children as they are ordinarily known—
unstable, lazy, disorderly, violent, stubborn, dis-
obedient, etc.—are "functionally" ill and can be
cured by a hygienic form of psychic life. In other
words, they can be "normalized." Then they become
like the disciplined children who gave those revelations
at the beginning of our work and who surprised us so
much. In consequence of this normalization the children
do not become "obedient to a teacher who gives them
lessons and corrects them," but they find their guide in
the laws of nature, i.e.; they start again to function
normally. Then they can reveal to us by their outer
behavior that kind of *psychic physiology*, which, like the
physiology of the body, functions *within*, in the complicated labyrinth of the soul. What is usually called the
Montessori Method revolves around this essential point.

We can affirm with certainty, after more than forty
years of experience and from repeated proofs obtained
among all races all over the world, that spontaneous
discipline was the basis on which rested all the other

astonishing results, as for example, the explosion into writing and all those other forms of progress that became evident later.

First "normal functioning" must be obtained—a "state of health"—and the establishment of this is what we call "normalization."

If the child is to advance, it is necessary that he first normalize himself, just like a sick man who cannot produce work according to his native endowments unless he first recovers his health.

What psychoanalysts try to do is precisely to "normalize" the adults who find so many difficulties in their activity, in their efforts to achieve their social purpose. In clinics for difficult children the same thing is attempted, viz., to bring their functions back to a state of normality.

Let us now suppose that a method of education recognizes that it is necessary to normalize a child right from the beginning and then to keep alive the natural continuation of this state of normality. That method would then have for its foundation a kind of "psychic hygiene," which helps men to grow up in good mental health.

This does not touch philosophical theories regarding the good or evil nature of man—not even the lofty abstract idea of what "normal man" really is. It is a practical fact and endeavor that can be applied universally.

The Basis of Growth

It is all very clear really. A subconscious impulse during the period of growth—that is of the construction of the individual—urges him to realize his growth, and the child is supremely happy when he is simply given the opportunity of doing this and of responding to his urge to make the greatest effort to achieve this. It can be said that the period of childhood is an age of "inner life" that leads to the developing, maturing, and perfecting of all the faculties. The outer world has value only insomuch as it offers the necessary means to reach the goal set by nature. That is why the child does not desire anything but what is adapted to his needs and uses it only as long as it helps him to achieve his aim.

Just as the child does not envy a child older than he, so also he does not desire things that are of no use to him at that particular time.

Hence we observe that peaceful and joyful attitude of the child who, in a favorable environment, chooses his objects and occupations.

The older child cannot inspire the younger one with a desire for competition; on the contrary, this latter's attitude is one of admiration and devotion. In the older child he sees an image of his own future triumph that is a certainty because the child will grow if he does not die. The older child does not arouse envy merely by being older.

Those feelings that could be called "bad" do not therefore appear. The naughtiness of small children is a manifestation of defense or of unconscious despair at not being able to "function" during that period on which the whole future depends and every hour of which brings its progress. Naughtiness can also be a form of agitation caused by mental hunger when the child is deprived of the stimuli of the environment or by a sense of frustration experienced when he is prevented from acting in the environment. The "unconscious aim" then moving ever further from its realization creates a kind of hell in the life of the child who becomes separated from a leading source and its creative energies.

It is only much later that envy at the success of others can arise, when the time for "drawing the first sketch of man" is over, and the child, who has been more or less successful in realizing the design of life, begins to be *interested in outer things* as such. Things are different then, and judgment with regard to "good and evil" can thus be made. Then we may speak of defects of a moral order concerning society, and the corrective intervention of education can be justified.

Expansive Education

The usual conception of direct correction and suppression of defects is wrong even at this stage. Correction is possible only by expansion, by giving "space," by opening up the means for the expansion of the personality. Wider interests than those observed in another individual at our side must be aroused. Only the poor quarrel over a piece of bread. The rich are attracted by the possibilities offered to them by the world. Envy and competition are signs of a "restricted mental development," of a limited outlook. He who has a vision of a "paradise" to be conquered cannot be satisfied by the whole world, and he easily renounces transitory and limited possessions.

The same applies to an education that "amplifies" and leads the individual beyond immediate interests. Envy and struggle are roused by the limitation of what can be conquered. A vast space gives different sentiments—sentiments that engender a passionate devotion for what makes for real progress.

An education of "vastness" therefore is the platform whereon certain moral defects can be eliminated. The first step of education must be to "extend the world" in which the child of today languishes, and its fundamental technique consists in "freeing him from the shackles that hinder him from going ahead." We must "multiply the motives of interest that satisfy the deepest tendencies buried in the soul and bring them within his reach. Invite him to conquer without limits, instead of repressing the desire to possess what belongs to those around him." On this plane, open to the realization of all possibilities, we can, and must, teach respect for the outer laws, established by that other natural power—the society of men.

In conclusion, the moral question, and hence that of moral goodness, cannot be discussed with regard to the "small child." Only when the child comes to the use of reason is it possible to bring the problems of philosophy into the field. Moral philosophers, however, deal with evil in much the same way—by directing the individual to transcend its appeals, with the aim of reaching God. In fact those who desire to fight against Original Sin do so by turning man towards the greatness of the Redemption.

2

Prejudices Regarding the Child in Science and Education

The Acquisition of Culture

In our schools where this educational experience has continued its progress, certain natural tendencies to "extend" culture and "increase knowledge" have become evident in practice. They seem, indeed, to follow the path of nature. The problems of teaching seem to be reversed there. It appears that the practical problem of the teacher is not to impart knowledge within fixed limits but rather to "restrain" and "direct" the children in their eagerness to learn ever more, as one has to tame spirited young horses. What is necessary is a guide for this holding back and not whips to make them go on.

The very way of transmitting culture is different. The *technique* of teaching in ordinary schools is a slow successive progress along supposed difficulties, which are graded and classified in advance. Children left free in their prepared environment, on the contrary, revealed original *techniques* that we could not have suspected.

The child really learns only when he can exercise his own energies according to the mental procedure of nature, and he sometimes acts very differently from what is ordinarily supposed. That is why he fails and hides himself under the treatment used in ordinary schools. The child can show his surprising achievements only if the adult applies the scientific technique of "indirect intervention" while helping the natural development of the child.

The precocious and extensive cultural progress revealed by our children, which called forth such admiration but also such opposition based on misunderstanding and a lack of understanding, rests on a principle referring to the psychology of the child. This is, that the child learns by his own activity, taking culture from the environment and not from the teacher, and further, as can now be satisfactorily proved, by putting into action also the powers of the subconscious that remain free to absorb and express according to the natural processes of the absorbent mind.

It will be said that the adult forms part of the environment, and in fact he intervenes by helping this natural process; yet the fact remains that the child cannot, as is generally believed, learn only through the efforts of the teacher who explains things, be he the most excellent and perfect of teachers. Also, in learning the child follows inner laws of mental formation. There is a direct interchange between the child and his environment, while the adult, with his offerings of motives of interest and his initiations, constitutes primarily a link, a *trait d'union*, between them.

The process of learning has been gone into, ever more deeply since our experiences were intensified, with the intention of knowing these phenomena more intimately. It was found among many children placed in suitable conditions that they were passionately interested in mathematics, in big numbers, and not only in big arithmetical operations, but also in calculations on quite a superior level, like those on the powers of numbers, the extraction of square and cubic roots—and especially in geometrical problems. We also discovered their capacity for learning several languages at the same time, studying the grammar and style of each. There was for example an eight-year-old child in India who took great interest in reading Sanskrit poetry, though Sanskrit is a dead language. He translated Vedic stories from Hindi into English although his mother tongue was Gujarati—another Indian language. His culture, therefore, extended from living and dead languages to those of a foreign country.

To this may be added their interest in natural science, their prodigious memory for names, and curiously enough, their delight in learning complicated systems of classification of plants and animals. These classifications are often not only uncertain but seem to encumber the memory unnecessarily. Official science is therefore thinking of abolishing them at least from school syllabuses, considering them as demanding useless effort.

This interest in classifications revealed itself with the help of moveable symbols. The pleasure experienced by children when they could create a mental order among these pictures and put each in its own place was very evident. It certainly was not an exercise of the memory, but one of construction, similar to that of a small child who plays with wet sand. The many ideas and names, which would otherwise be "lost" to the memory, are gathered and captured in a fascinating construction. It is rather like the mathematical apparatus that is built up in the exercises of the decimal system, where units are gathered in such clear successive hierarchies that arithmetic is almost a consequence of the order of units. Thus it happens also with historical events placed in relation to their dates and to geography that constructs in the mind a system of cultural facts in time and space.

The creative forces of nature also proceed in this way. In the construction of the mother tongue by the child, language is initially built up on the sounds of words and on grammar, i.e., the order in which the words have to be placed to express thought. This is the first fundamental construction that is completed shortly after the child has reached two years of age, while the number of words is still comparatively small. Afterwards language is enriched spontaneously by new words that find their places in the order already established.

We found that the procedure adopted by us with children under nine years of age could be applied to those of more advanced age, and we can affirm that at all stages of school life it is essential that no obstruction be placed in the way of the individual activity of the children in course of development. Only thus can they obey the "natural process of psychic development." It is true that the teacher or lecturer has an ever more important role to play as culture reaches higher levels, but this role consists rather in stimulating interest than in actual teaching. When children are interested in a subject they tend to spend a long time studying it, or in other words, trying to find their way in it until they reach a kind of "maturity" by means of their own experience. After that an acquisition has not only been made, but it tends to extend itself ever further. The poor teacher then finds himself compelled to go beyond the limits he had put to his own teaching. His difficulty then does not lie in how to "make the pupils learn" but in knowing how to meet unexpected claims on the part of his pupils, in having to teach, then and there, things he never intended to teach. Instruction, in other words, tends to extend of its own accord. Often, after a long rest, say a vacation, the children do not merely retain what they had previously learned, but their culture seems to be richer, as if by magic. After the holidays they know more than before. Their power to absorb from the environment has therefore been reawakened.

The procedure of spontaneous activity consists sometimes in a voluntarily intensified and complicated effort that absorbs all their mental energies for hours on end and even during several consecutive days. I remember a child who wanted to draw a river—the Rhine—with all its tributaries. He had, therefore, to search a long time in geographical treatises that had nothing to do with schoolbooks. For the actual drawing he chose graph paper as used by engineers and made use of compasses and various other instruments. He succeeded in his endeavor showing tremendous patience—nobody, surely, would ever have exacted such an effort from him.

Another time I saw a boy who had resolved to work out a gigantic multiplication of a number consisting of 30 figures by another of 25 figures. The partial products accumulated to such an extent that the boy was surprised. He had to have recourse to the help of two friends, who had to find sheets of paper and stick them together to contain this monstrous operation and its enormous development. After two consecutive days of work the multiplication was not yet finished. It was completed only the next day, yet without the boys showing any sign of being tired of it. They, too, seemed proud of and satisfied with their great achievement.

Again, I remember four or five children who decided to carry out together the algebraic multiplication of the whole alphabet by itself—to work out the square of the alphabet. This time also the operation required the material effort of sticking together ever more strips of paper, which in all reached a length of about ten meters.

These patient endeavors lead to a strengthening of the mind and rendered it more agile, as gymnastic training does to the body.

One child acquired the capacity to carry out quite complicated operations with fractions without writing them down. He thus showed his ability to retain in his mind the image of the numbers and the successive operations. While the child carried out these operations mentally, a teacher did so on paper, not being able to do them otherwise. At the end of his calculation the child announced his result. The teacher (who was in charge of a number of English schools and had come to visit our schools in Holland) remarked that the result given by the child was not correct. The child, without being perturbed in the least, thought for a while and then said, "Yes, I see where I made a mistake," and gave the correct result a little while later. This subsequent mental correction in quite a complicated calculation caused greater astonishment than the fact that he had been able to carry out the operation itself. The mind of the child, evidently, possessed a peculiar faculty for retaining all these successive phases.

Yet another time, there was a child who had learned the extraction of the square root according to the procedure indicated by our apparatus. He was intensely interested in extracting such roots by himself, but he did so in a different way invented by himself, which, however, he could not explain.

We could go on giving endless examples. One of the most extraordinary ones was the patient work of a boy who wrote down the grammatical analysis of a whole booklet. He never interrupted this work until it was completed and spent several days doing nothing else.

These psychic manifestations reveal a kind of formative mechanism expressed by exercises without any outer utility, without any practical applicability. It would not be possible to impose them as one could do in physical drill because it would be impossible to sustain from without such a lively and uninterrupted interest, such a constant attention for things that in themselves are not very attractive and rather purposeless.

They require really a spontaneous effort such as would be impossible to inspire from without. Notwithstanding such a "waste of time" shown by so many children in various occupations, these same children make exceptional progress in all the branches of culture and also in art. In a school in India, where there was a special teacher for music and dancing, a group of children often gathered in the music room when that teacher was not there and improvised dances that the teacher had not taught them. They differed very much from the rigidly prescribed movements of classical Indian dancing. Various children would play on instruments rhythms that accompanied a kind of choral singing invented by themselves. All showed an intense interest that was more than mere delight. From time to time these unexpected forms of music were heard in the school.

We encounter here phenomena very different from those considered in ordinary education and in educational psychology, which is concerned only with will and effort. These are considered as results of reflection of the intellect or of external compulsion. Here, however, we witness a kind of élan vital, an eruption of unforeseen and unsuspected manifestations that have nothing to do with reflection nor with any practical or utilitarian application. Nevertheless, progress in a real acquisition of culture is evidently much more helped by these inner energies than by a voluntary and imposed effort. The results thus obtained are not directly related to these strange exercises of patience and this constant work. They seem to belong rather to inner mechanisms that by their action give an impulse to the development of the personality as a whole.

In fact one of its most indirect consequences is the formation of "character." The children not only make progress in a marvelous acquisition of culture, but they acquire more mastery of their actions, more assuredness in their behavior, without any stiffening or any hesitation due to timidity or fear. They are also ready to adapt themselves to other people and to the environment and its different exigencies. Joy in life, together with discipline, seems to be the result of their activities guided from within rather than from any outer circumstances. On this basis, the children are then ready to master the environment. As they are more balanced and more capable of orienting and valuing themselves, they are characteristically calm and serene and for that reason also easily adapt themselves to other people.

In the course of our experiences we were met with crushing opposition by prejudices on this point also. Although all complained of the lack of culture and emphasized its absolute necessity for civilized life in our times, there was great opposition to the development of culture in our schools. It seemed almost as if the child had to be defended against us. The force of mental inertia considered these revelations of the children almost as a pedagogical and still more as a psychological heresy and vigorously opposed the presentation of our apparatus that helped such development. The discoveries of mental *surménage*, strain, among children in ordinary schools were brought into the field, and we were accused of forcing the intellectual energies of the child. Our so-called intellectualism was denounced, while we ourselves were absolutely innocent of it all.

The simple facts, of which we have related but a few, surprised us as much as they did others, but in the case of these latter, their surprise was mixed with suspicion. Who would ever have pretended to evoke the manifestation of these powers in the children? Certainly not I! The children themselves revealed them, and we did nothing but respect them in the atmosphere of the freedom of our schools. We responded only with the help they sought. We did, however, make an attempt to understand the source of these powers and to investigate the conditions that permitted and maybe facilitated their "eruption." Only the universal repetition of the same phenomena, among children of so many different races and of civilizations so much more primitive than ours, compelled us to conclude that we were face-to-face with "normal" possibilities, with truly human powers, which all too long had remained hidden on account of a lack of respect on the part of the adult for the laws of psychic development. They had remained unknown because the adult had denied them the help that it is their right to claim from education.

The Social Question of the Child

The results we have touched upon are not easy to obtain because enormous obstacles are encountered in century-old prejudices. The field of child life and child education is one in which all have had experience right from the beginning of man's appearance on earth and in which they continue to have experience. These experiences have had a long time to consolidate and to become universal. Unfortunately there are also modern branches of science or attempts at science that have developed around the most superficial manifestations of child behavior (actually around the "effects" of outer circumstances) and these reached an easy compromise with those prejudices that every adult cherishes regarding the child. That is why the manifestations of child life that we mentioned are not observed by people "who have eyes and see," but rather by those already blinded by prejudice.

These prejudices are so universal that it is difficult to have them recognized as such. They are confused and strengthened by the evidence of facts because all, or nearly all, see the child as he is commonly known, not the child as he is, still an unknown entity. In fact, if one should tell an audience that in order to reform education many prejudices have to be overcome, the most progressive and unbiased among the listeners would think at once of prejudices relating to what has, or has not, to be taught and not of prejudices regarding the child himself. They think that it is a question of removing prejudices and errors from what is taught so as not to transmit them to the younger generation. Some hold that the teaching of dogmatic religious conceptions should be avoided; others, that certain unsocial class distinctions should be removed; others again, that certain formal habits no longer belonging to our society should be eliminated; and so on.

It seems, however, as yet inconceivable that there are prejudices that "prevent" us from seeing the child from a point of view different from that which is usually taken when looking at him.

Yet those who study child psychology and education must take into account not those social prejudices that bother modern educators so much, but *other* prejudices—those that concern the child *directly*, his natural attributes and powers, the abnormal conditions of his life.

By removing religious prejudice, it may perhaps be possible to understand better the greatness or significance of religions but not the natural personality of the child. By removing prejudices concerning social castes, it may be possible to intensify the understanding and harmony between the members of society, but it will not help to a better understanding of the child. If many formalities in our social relations are recognized to be futile, belonging to the past, we may witness a reform of social customs, but we will not understand the child any better.

All that seems to contribute to social progress among adults can, according to common opinion, leave the vital necessities of childhood aside. The adult has always seen only himself in society and in its progress. The child has remained outside society—an unknown quantity in the equation of life!

Hence a prejudice has found its way into the adult —the notion that the life of the child can be changed or improved only through teaching. This prejudice impedes the understanding of the fact that the child constructs himself, that he has a *teacher within* himself, and that this inner teacher also follows a program and a technique of education, and that we adults by acknowledging this unknown teacher may enjoy the privilege and good fortune of becoming his assistants and faithful servants, by helping him with our cooperation.

Many other prejudices are the logical consequences of this one. It is said that the mind of a child is empty—without a guide and without laws of its own. Adults, therefore, are supposed to have the great and complete responsibility of filling it, guiding, and commanding it. It is believed that the child is naturally inclined towards a number of defects, towards decadence, and inertia; that by nature he is blown hither and thither as a feather driven before the wind; and that adults, therefore, must stimulate and encourage him, correct and guide him all the time.

In the same way it is assumed in the physical order that the child cannot control his movements and is incapable of taking care of himself, and so the adult hurries to do everything for him without bothering to consider that the child can very well manage alone. The child is then said to be a heavy burden and a great responsibility because he requires this constant care. The attitude of the adult to the child is that he must "create" in him a grown-up man and that the intelligence, the socially useful activity, the character of this human being who has entered his home, are all his work.

Then pride is born as an accompaniment to this anxiety and sense of responsibility. The child seen in this light owes infinite respect and gratitude to his creators, his saviours. If instead he rebels, he must be corrected, must be brought into submission with the help of violence, if necessary. In order to be perfect the child must then be perfectly passive and most rigorously obedient. He is a perfect parasite of his parents, and as long as they assume the whole economical burden of his life, he must depend upon them absolutely. He is a "child." Even when he has grown up and has to shave regularly each morning before attending the university, he still remains dependent upon his father and teachers just as when he was still a child. He must go where his father wishes him to go, study as often as his teachers and professors wish him to study. He will remain outside society even when he takes his degree and may be twenty-six years of age.

He cannot marry without his father's consent until quite an advanced age that has been fixed, not in consideration of his needs and sentiments, but by a social law promulgated by the adults and equal for all.

He must actually obey unto death when society tells him, "Parasite, prepare yourself to kill or be killed!" If he does not do that, if he does not render military service, he will be ostracized from society and classed as a delinquent.

All this runs through our world like the quiet water of a brook through a meadow. This is the preparation for life given to a man; and as for women, they are still more dependent and condemned for life.

The norms of this way of life form the basis of society. Nobody may be called *good* who does not submit to them.

Thus from birth onwards and until all the rules

dictated by the adult have been followed, the child and youth are not considered as *men* in society. They are exemplified by those young students who are told: "Think of your studies. Do not occupy yourselves with politics and ideas different from those that have been imposed upon you. You have no civil rights."

The social world is opened only after this kind of dictatorial preparation.

We must admit that some evolution has taken place during the history of civilization. While Roman law recognized the father as master of his family with the right to kill his children as he created them by a right of nature and while, in those days, weak or deformed children were destroyed by being thrown down a steep rock (the Tarpeian rock), which fulfilled the function of purging the race, Christianity, on the other hand, placed one's own child and the deformed child under a law of respect for life. That, however, is all. The child can no longer be killed.

Slowly science, in the shape of hygiene, has succeeded in "protecting" the life of the child against disease and evident cruelty. It has, however, taken great care not to dictate how to reform social conditions so that the life of *all* children, and not of the diseased ones only, be protected.

The personality of the child has remained buried under the prejudices of order and justice. Though the adult has agitated very strongly in defense of his own rights, he has overlooked those of the child. He is not even aware of him. On this plane, life has continued to evolve and to complicate itself up to the present century.

From the complex whole of such conceptions arise

the particular prejudices that impose themselves under the cloak of so praiseworthy an aim as the protection of and respect for the life of childhood.

The small child, for example, should not be allowed to do any form of *work*. He must be abandoned to a life of intellectual inertia. He should only play in a certain well-established way.

If, therefore, one day it is discovered that the child is a great worker, who can apply himself to his work even with concentration, who can learn by himself, teach himself, and who possesses discipline within himself, this seems to be like a fairy tale. It does not evoke surprise; it appears only utterly absurd.

No attention is paid to this *reality*, and hence no conclusion is reached to the effect that in this apparent contradiction may be hidden an *error* on the part of the adult. It is simply impossible; it cannot exist —or as it is said, it is not serious.

The greatest difficulty in the way of an attempt to give freedom to the child and to bring his powers to light does not lie in finding a form of education that realizes these aims. It lies rather in overcoming the prejudices that the adult has formed in his regard. That is why I said we must recognize, investigate, and fight against "the prejudices concerning the child" only, without touching other prejudices that the adult may have formed regarding his own life.

This struggle against prejudices is the social question of the child that must accompany the renewal of his education. It is, in other words, imperative to prepare a positive and well-defined *route* leading to this goal. If the prejudices concerning the child are directly and *exclusively* aimed at, a *reform of the adult* will accompany it step by step because an obstacle in the adult will have been removed. This reform of the adult is of enormous importance for society as a whole. It represents the reawakening of a part of human consciousness that has been covering itself progressively with layer upon layer of impediments. Moreover, without this reawakening all other social questions become obscure and the problems raised by them insoluble. "Consciousness" has been dimmed, not only in some adults but in all adults—because all have dealings with children. As their consciousness is dimmed regarding the child, they also act unconsciously. On this point they do not use their powers of reflection, their intelligence that leads them to make progress in other fields. There is in them, as we already mentioned, a *blind spot*, similar to that on the retina of the eye. The child, that unknown being, that only apparently human being, sometimes considered almost as a matrimonial accident who opens a road of sacrifices and duties, does not in himself arouse either awe or admiration.

Let me describe a psychological complex. Suppose that in nature the child appeared as a divine miracle, just as men feel in the presence of the image of the Child Jesus, who inspires artists and poets and who is the hope of redemption for all mankind, an august figure at whose feet the kings of the East and West devoutly place their gifts. This Child Jesus is, however, in the religious worship paid to Him also, a real child, a newly-born babe without consciousness. Almost all parents do feel such lofty sentiments at the birth of their child, who is idealized by the strength of their love. Later, however, as this child grows up, he begins to be a nuisance. Almost remorsefully, they begin to defend themselves against him. They are happy when he is asleep and try to make him sleep as long as possible. Those who can, hand their child over to the care of a nurse and, taking courage, instruct her to keep him away from them as much as possible. If this unknown and incomprehensible being, acting in obedience to unconscious urges, does not submit, he is punished, fought against, and being weak and defenseless, both intellectually and physically, he must bear all. In the adult's soul there occurs a "conflict" because he does love the child. At first this conflict causes pain and remorse. Later, however, the psychic mechanism at play between the conscious and subconscious in man reaches a form of adaptation. As Freud would say, there occurs a fugue. The subconscious prevails, i.e., it suggests, "What you do is not in order to defend yourself against the child, it is a duty you perform in his regard. It is a necessary good. You must even act bravely because you are 'educating' the child. You are striving to build up goodness in him." When this comfort is obtained, the natural feelings of admiration and love are effectively buried.

This is seen in all, because this phenomenon belongs to human nature. Thus a kind of "subconscious organization of defense" is achieved by all parents in the world. All lean upon each other. The whole of society forms a collective subconscious, wherein all act in complete agreement when they remove and suppress the child. They all act for his good, they all perform a duty towards him, nay, even a sacrifice. In this way, that kind of remorse, which was there originally, is sacrificed. In this conflict it remains definitively buried under the solidarity of adult society. What has thus been established assumes the power of suggestion and the appearance of an absolute truth on which all agree. Future parents, in their turn, are subjected to this suggestion and prepared for the duties and sacrifices they will have to perform for the future well-being of their children.

These people, who are victims of suggestion, prepare their consciousness for such an adaptation, and the child is buried in the subconscious. As in all people who are victims of suggestion, in these too, there exists henceforth only what has been established by suggestion. This state of affairs is perpetuated from generation to generation.

In the course of ages, the child, buried as he is, will no longer be able to reveal anything of his lofty nature.

We have given a kind of formula—an acronym—to indicate this phenomenon. What is believed to be good is in reality disguised evil. This evil has organized itself and has found a subconscious solution for grave conflicts. Nobody desires evil, all desire good, but that "good" is evil. Everyone has been infected by it through the suggestion coming from the morally uniform environment. In society, therefore, an *O*rganization of Evil (*M*ale) has been formed, which assumes the semblance of Good (*B*ene), and is *I*mposed on the whole of h*U*manity by *S*uggestion; when we combine the initials of these characteristic words and form a word, we then get: OMBIUS.

The OMBIUS

The social *ombius* dominates the child. All submit to it instead of seeing the sublime child as the little brother of the Child Jesus. *Ombiotic* feelings fatally cover the life of the child while a luminously ideal figure of him remains as a symbol only on the altars of religion.

When adults come to the sincere conclusion that all are children of God and that Christ lives in each one of them and He becomes their model for imitation, or better still, for identification with Him to the extent of being able to say: "I live now, not I, but Christ liveth in me," they except the child. The Child Jesus remains separate from the poor newly born, who is buried under the *ombius*. In him, people see only the original sin that must be fought against.

This short illustration based on the psychological secrets of human nature shows the primordial reality of a growing and total oppression of the child. The prejudice of the whole of society, organized by the adults, weighs upon him, although he is isolated in the family. In the course of evolution and the successive social movements for the rights of man, the child is forgotten.

The history of the injustices committed against the child has not yet been written officially and is, therefore, not taught as part of the history studied in schools of any grade. Even students who take a specialized degree in this subject have never heard it mentioned. History deals only with the adult because only he exists in our consciousness. Similarly, those who specialize in legal studies learn a number of laws both of the present and past, but they never become aware that no laws have been promulgated on behalf of the child's rights. Civilization ignores a question that has never yet become a "social problem."

Yet the child is taken into consideration when he can be of use to the adult, but even then he continues to touch the blind spot of consciousness as far as his destiny as a *human being* is concerned.

Let us take the most evident example. At the time of the French Revolution the Rights of Man were proclaimed for the first time. Among these was included the right of all men to be taught how to read and write. What was until then a privilege most readily accessible only to members of the better classes became now a universal right. It would have been logical had all adults availed themselves of this opportunity even though it entailed an effort, because here was a right that not only did away with exclusive privileges but also implied an effort to improve the individual.

However, the burden of this was laid only on the children. On them the whole burden of the effort required to make this conquest was laid.

Thus, we see here, for the first time in history, a "mobilization" of children, both boys and girls. All were equally called up for service in the schools, as in time of war manhood is mobilized for military service in the field.

We all know the lamentable story. The child was condemned to a life sentence because for the whole of his life as a child he was sent to prison. Locked up within bare cells, kept sitting on wooden benches, under the sway of a tyrant who insisted that the children even think as he wished, learn what he wished, and do what he wished. The delicate hand of the child was made to write. His mind, full of imaginative powers, had to concentrate on the dry shapes of the alphabet that did not reveal to him any of the advantages that its possession confers upon us. These advantages are discovered only by the adult.

What a history of unrecorded martyrdom! Children were tortured—their fingers tied to penholders; they were beaten with rods and forced to a cruel exercise. The sufferings of these little prisoners are too well known—even their spinal cords were twisted and deformed because they were condemned to sit on a wooden bench for hours on end, day after day, year after year, and that during the delicate years of early growth.

Herded together, exposed to the promiscuousness of diseases, suffering from the cold—it was thus children had to live in those concentration camps. This lasted up to our century. The advantage derived from this situation was a right belonging to the adult, not to the child. Nobody, however, felt any gratitude towards him, nobody tried to alleviate his sufferings. Yet there always lived on in parents those natural feelings of parental love that they showed at the birth of their child. Always too there were those instincts for the protection of the young, common even to animals.

How can this be explained except by a mysterious phenomenon in our consciousness? What could explain better than this example the reality of the *ombius* and the prejudices concerning the child?

Now in our century a serious effort is being made to alleviate those sufferings. An attempt is being made to transform education. More healthy and beautiful schools are being built. All this, however, is being effected around the same figure of the misunderstood child who is still seen through eyes distorted by the *ombius*.

3

The "Nebulae"

Man and Animals

Only when we logically consider, from the point of view of heredity, the newly born human child do we see that he differs from the newly born of mammals. The young of mammals inherit, as all animals generally do, a specialized behavior. This is as fixed as the morphological features of their body. The bodily form is precisely suited to the functions it has to perform in life. These functions are fixed for each species. The habits, the way of moving, whether of skipping, running, or climbing, are established from birth onwards. Their adaptation to the environment, therefore, aims at exercising characteristic functions, the purpose of which is not merely to preserve the species, but further to contribute to the total functioning of nature, which is their cosmic purpose. The legs of those that jump, run, climb, or dig into the earth are formed in such a way as to correspond to the task of each. Also ferocity or the avidity to feed on corpses and offal contribute to the cosmic order on the surface of the earth. In short, the body, in its fleetness or rigidity, is built so that the "cosmic aim" of each individual species may be fulfilled. The species endowed with the power of some particular limited variability of innate adaptation are very few. Those species have all been domesticated by man. The greater part of the animals preserve an absolute rigidity in their hereditary characteristics and cannot be domesticated.

Man, on the contrary, has an almost unlimited power of adaptation as regards his capacity to live in all geographical regions and his capacity to assume innumerable forms of habit and work. Man, in fact, belongs to the only species capable of an indefinite evolution in its activities in the outer world. From this flows the development of civilization. The human species is the only one that by nature is not fixed in its behavior as all other species are. It is, as biologists recently asserted, a species in a perpetual state of infancy, because it develops in continuous progress.

This, therefore, is the first difference—man does not receive as inheritance a fixed behavior.

Another evident difference is that no young of a mammal is born as inert, as incapable of actualizing the characteristics of the adults of its species, as is the newly born human being. Many animals such as kids, foals, and calves stand on their own legs almost at once, and during the period of lactation they run after their mothers.

Even monkeys, which are considered nearest to

man, are vivacious and intelligent as soon as they are born. They cling energetically of their own strength to their mothers and need not be carried in their arms. The mother monkey climbs trees while her young holds onto her, gripping her tightly with its little arms. Not only that, but often the young one tries to run away, and the mother must make an effort to catch it and keep it with her.

The human child, instead, is inert for a long time. He does not speak, whereas all other young creatures at once begin to chirp or bark or reproduce the sounds peculiar to their species. All dogs the world over, of whatever breed they may be, bark. All cats meow, just as all birds have their peculiar cries and songs—a form of expression belonging to the characteristics of their species.

The long inertia and incapacity of the child belong truly to the human species alone. At an age when a bull is capable of reproduction, although it has a body so much larger than that of a man and more or less the same physiological organs, the child is still a mere child, far from maturity.

Those who study only the evolution of the morphological form and its respective organs in order to deduce from it the direct descent of man from animals, have, however, given insufficient attention to the *differences* that are thrown into relief by this mysterious feature of the length of human childhood. Thus a void remains, which the theories regarding evolution have not yet considered.

It would, in fact, seem possible to agree on a logical basis that man is physically an ape, evolved by means of long efforts at adaptation to the environment and through those efforts only, because there is an evident similarity between the body of man and that of the ape. The face and skull of a primitive man resemble very much those of a superior ape. The limbs and generally the skeletons of both are surprisingly similar. Those who think that primitive man had also to climb trees like a monkey are merely insisting on a commonplace that has been fantastically elaborated in the motion pictures of Tarzan. Yet one thing remains inexplicable. We can imagine a primitive man of low morphological type who climbed trees, but we cannot admit that such men had newly born infants who spoke, clung to their mothers of their own strength, got to their feet and immediately started to run about! It is difficult to give a reason why man as he evolved to superior types of life, i.e., towards the species of the Homo sapiens, should see his infants become passive, dumb, deprived of intelligence, and for years on end incapable of achieving what he could do in previous stages of evolution! One of the characteristics, therefore, of human beings, which is distinctly different from those found elsewhere, resides in the newly born child.

It does not matter that today we cannot explain this fact. The fact is there and makes it easy to argue that, if the newly born child of man is so evidently and greatly inferior to that of the mammals, he must have a special function that the others do not share.

This function does not come from the inheritance of previous infantile forms. It is, therefore, related to some new character that has risen during the process of evolution.

This character cannot be recognized by observing the adult human being, but it is clearly seen by observing the child.

Something *new* occurred during the evolutionary process that led to the realization of man, just as new characteristics also occurred in the animal world when, after the reptiles, birds, and mammals came into existence, i.e., warm blood and an instinctive care for the preservation of the species. The true difference between birds and reptiles does not lie in eventual teeth in the beak of the archaeopteryx, or the long tail made up of many vertebrae, but in the parental love that did not exist before and that appears together with the warm blood. There are, therefore, *additions* in evolution, not merely transformations.

The Function of the Child

The child must have a special function besides being merely smaller and weaker than the adult. He does not possess "by birth" all the attributes that are destined to increase and grow within him as a means to attain adulthood. Actually, if he already possessed such fixed features, as happens in other species, man could never adapt himself to such different places and habits, nor evolve in his social manners, nor take up such different forms of work.

He is, therefore, different from animals precisely with regard to heredity. He evidently does not inherit *characteristic features*, but only the potentiality to form them. It is, therefore, *after birth* that the characteristics, proper to the particular kind to which the child belongs, are built up.

Let us take language as an example. It is certain

that man must possess and transmit hereditarily the completely new faculty of developing a language that is in relation to the intelligence and the necessity of transmitting thought for the purpose of social co-operation. Yet there does not exist any *particular language* that is thus transmitted. Man does not "speak a language" merely because he grows, as a puppy barks wherever in the world it is found, even if isolated from other dogs. Language is developed gradually, precisely during that epoch of inertia and unconsciousness of early infancy. At two years or two years and three months, the child speaks distinctly and reproduces precisely the language spoken in his environment. He does not by heredity reproduce the language of his father and mother. In fact, if a child is taken from his parents and people and reared in another country where another language is spoken, he will reproduce the language of the place where he lives. If an Italian baby is taken to the United States, he will speak English with an American accent and will not know Italian. It is, therefore, the child himself who assumes a language, and until he acquires it he is dumb in contrast to the young of other animals.

Those "jungle children," of whom history speaks, were children found abandoned in the forest. Through exceptional circumstances they had survived abandonment in the midst of wild animals, and they were *mute* even at the age of twelve or sixteen years when they were first discovered. None of them reproduced the cries of the animals among which they had lived and by which they were adopted in a certain sense. The famous savage of Aveyron was mute when he was found and then educated by the French physician Itard, who discovered that the boy was neither deaf nor incapable of speech. In fact he learned to speak French and also to read and write it. He had remained deaf and dumb in appearance only because he had been living far from man—from people who did speak.

Language, therefore, is developed *ex novo* by the child himself. He develops it naturally, of course, but that means only that he has inherited the power to do so. Yet it is the child who develops it in himself, taking it from the environment. Nothing is more interesting than the recent psychological studies based on the exact observation of the development of language in the child. Children absorb, unconsciously of course, language in a grammatical way. While they remain apparently inert for a long time, all of a sudden, within about two years and three months, they reveal a phenomenon—the explosion of a language already wholly formed.

There was, therefore, an *inner development* during the long period when the baby was unable to express himself. He was actually elaborating in the mysterious recesses of his unconscious mind a whole language with the grammatical order of words necessary to express thought. This children achieve with regard to all possible languages. The simple, such as those spoken by certain African tribes, and the most complicated, such as German or Russian, all are absorbed in exactly the same period of time. In every race the child begins to speak at about two years of age and it was certainly so in the past also. Thus,

Roman children must have spoken Latin with its complicated cases and declensions, which cause so much trouble to youths of our time who have to learn it in secondary schools. Formerly in India, small children must have spoken Sanskrit, which students of today find almost insurmountably difficult.

The Tamil language of South India is very difficult for us, with its almost imperceptible sounds and accents where the meaning of the sentence is changed by merely raising or lowering the voice a bit. Yet, small children of two years of age in the villages and plains of India speak this Tamil.

Similarly, one of the difficulties of those who study Italian is to remember the gender of nouns because not only is there no hard-and-fast rule governing it, but many nouns are masculine in the singular and feminine in the plural or vice versa, so it is almost impossible for a foreigner to avoid mistakes. Yet the ignorant urchins in the street never make mistakes and laugh at those of foreigners. Sometimes learned people who have made a real study of the Italian language and mastered all its rules and sounds, still have this remark made to them: "You have a foreign accent—what is your nationality?"

Languages absorbed in early childhood are evident and inimitable. They are our "mother tongue." They are the property of the ignorant as well as of the learned. The mother tongue is a unique language for each individual who possesses it, in its sounds, its intonation, and its grammatical construction. It indicates from what country one comes and to what race one belongs just as much as does the color of one's skin or one's bodily build.

How were those different languages fixed—those languages elaborated by infinite generations and those sounds evolved by the thought of man? Certainly not because the child gave them his conscious attention nor because he studied them intelligently. Man has as hereditary character the faculty of speech, but it is not by heredity that any particular language is transmitted. What then is transmitted?

A comparison could be made with the nebulae from which the heavenly bodies originated. These nebulae are almost unsubstantial masses of ethereal gases, without consistency, yet they slowly solidify, and transforming themselves become stars and planets.

If, in a comparison, we suppose an inheritance of language, it would be like an inconsistent, mute *nebula*, without which, nevertheless, there would be no possibility of developing any language. The nebulae are like mysterious potentialities comparable to those genes in the germinal cell that have power to direct the future tissues so that they can form complicated and structurally complete, determined organs.

The Spiritual Embryo

Could we not call the child, who in appearance only is psychically inert, an *embryo*, in whom the psychical powers and organs of man are being developed? He is an embryo in whom exists nothing but nebulae that have the power to develop spontaneously certainly, but only *at the expense of the environment—*

an environment rich in greatly different forms of civilization. That is why the human embryo must be *born* before completing itself and why it can reach further development only after birth. Its potentialities, in fact, must be stimulated by the environment.

There will be many "inner influences" just as in physical growth there are many, especially during the processes depending on the genes, e.g., the influence of various hormones. In the spiritual embryo, instead, there are directing *sensitivities*. In the case of language, the examination of the sense organs reveals that the sense of hearing seems to be the least developed during the first weeks of life. Yet the most delicate sounds that compose a word have to be received through that very sense. It appears, therefore, that the ear does not merely *hear* as a sense organ but is guided by special sensitivities to collect the sounds of human speech only from the environment. These sounds are not merely heard; they provoke motor reactions in the delicate fibres of the vocal chords—the tongues, lips, etc. Thus among all the muscle fibres it is those of the speech organs that are aroused to reproduce those sounds. Nevertheless, this is not immediately revealed but stored away until that time when language is to be born, just as the child during intrauterine life is being formed without functioning and is then, at a given moment, stimulated to enter the world and starts functioning all of a sudden.

These, of course, are suppositions, but the fact remains that there are inner developments, *directed* by creative energies, and that these developments can reach maturity before they become outwardly manifest.

When they finally reveal themselves they are *characteristics* already built up to form part of the individuality of the person.

The Absorbent Mind

Certainly these complicated processes do not at all follow the procedure established in the adult mind. The child has not learned a language as we would learn a foreign tongue by an effort of our conscious mental faculties. He has yet achieved an exact, firm, and marvelous construction like the embryonic constructions of an organ that forms part of a whole organism.

There exists in the small child an unconscious mental state that is of a creative nature. We have called it the "absorbent mind." This absorbent mind does not construct with a voluntary effort but according to the lead of "inner sensitivities," which we call "sensitive periods" as the sensitivity lasts only for a definite period, i.e., until the acquisition to be made according to natural development has been achieved. Thus if the nebula for language met with obstacles in its development and the constructive acoustic sensitivity did not function, a deaf-mute might be the result, though his organs of hearing and speech would be perfectly normal.

It is clear that there must be a secret fact in the psychic "creation" of man. If we learn everything through attention, volition, and intelligence, how then can the child undertake his great construction since he is not yet endowed with intelligence, willpower or attention? It is evident that in him there acts a mind totally different from ours and that, therefore, a psychic functioning, different from that of the conscious mind, can exist in the unconscious.

The acquisition of a language can serve as the most suitable example to give us an idea of this difference in mentality because language lends itself to study by direct and detailed observation.

The unconscious mind does not register any of the difficulties we experience with regard to different languages, which make us refer to some of them as easy and to others as extremely complicated. Evidently this absence of difficulties eliminates, therefore, gradual steps in the mastery of such difficulties. The *whole* language is taken in and always in the same period of time, independently of its simplicity or complication, as judged by the adult mind. This total acquisition of a language cannot be compared to the effort made by the *memory* when we learn a language, neither need we consider the lack of retentivity of the memory, which is evident in the case of the adult who easily lets his ephemeral acquisitions slip from him. In the period of unconscious activity language is indelibly stamped upon the mind and becomes a *characteristic* that man finds established in himself. No language that one may wish to add to the mother tongue can become a characteristic, and none will be so sure a possession as the first.

The case is very different with the adult who has to learn a language with his conscious mind. Evidently it is quite easy to learn a primitive language with a simple grammar, as some languages of the peoples of Central Africa are. They are often learned by missionaries during their journey across the ocean and deserts on their way to their destination. It is, on the contrary, very difficult to learn a complicated language like Latin, German, or Sanskrit. Students take four, five, or even eight years to study them, without knowing them perfectly even then. A living but foreign language is never entirely mastered—some grammatical mistake or "foreign accent" reveals that one is not speaking one's mother tongue. Furthermore, if this foreign language is not kept in continuous practice it is easily forgotten.

One's mother tongue is not entrusted to the conscious memory. It is deposited in a different memory similar to that which modern psychologists, biologists, and psychoanalysts call the "mneme" or "vital memory." It is supposed by some to contain what is transmitted by heredity through an infinity of time and is considered a "vital power."

A superficial comparison will, perhaps, illustrate this difference. Let us compare a photograph and a graphic reproduction made by the hand and intelligence together, in other words, by writing, drawing, or painting. A camera, with its sensitive film, can in a single instant take in anything that comes to it through light. There is no greater effort involved in taking a photograph of a whole forest than in taking that of an isolated tree. A group of people and their background are as easily photographed as a single face. Whatever the complication of the figure, the camera always takes it in the same way and in the same instantaneous flash —the fraction of a second when the shutter is opened and the light rays penetrate and reach the film. Whether one wishes to photograph the cover of a book with only its title on it or a full page covered with fine print, it is done in the same way, takes the same length of time, and produces an equally good result.

If, on the other hand, one wants to make a drawing, this is either easy or difficult according to the subject selected. The time required to reproduce a face in profile differs greatly from the time required to draw a full figure or a group of people or a landscape. A drawing, furthermore, never reproduces all the details even when we want it to do so; if a legal document regarding a subject or the position of a body is required, a photograph and not a drawing is demanded. In the same way, to copy the title of a book is easy enough and can be done quickly, but this is not the case in copying a closely written page. As the hand works on the object the slow progress made shows evidence of fatigue and of the successive efforts used. But the camera, after the picture is taken, remains as before and does not show anything of what happened. To obtain the picture, the film must be taken out in a dark place; it must be exposed to chemical agents that fix the image independently of the light that produced it. Once the image is fixed, the film can be washed and exposed to light because the image remains indelible and reproduces in all its details the object that was photographed.

It seems as if the absorbent mind acts in a like manner. There too the images must remain hidden in the darkness of the unconscious and have to be fixed by mysterious sensitivities while nothing yet appears outside. Only after this miraculous phenomenon has been accomplished will the creative acquisition be brought into the light of consciousness and there it remains indelible in all its particulars. In the case of language we witness an explosion shortly after two years of age, when the particular sounds, the prefixes and suffixes of words, their declension, the conjugation of the verbs, and the syntactical construction of the sentence are all there. This is then the indelible mother tongue, which has become a racial characteristic.

This absorbent mind is indeed a marvelous gift to humanity!

By merely "living" and without any conscious effort the individual absorbs from the environment even a complex cultural achievement like language. If this essential mental form existed in the adult, how much easier would our studies be! Let us imagine that we could go to another world, e.g., the planet Jupiter, and that we would find men there, who by merely walking about and living, absorbed all the sciences without ever studying them, who could acquire skills without any obvious exercise. We would surely exclaim, "How great and fortunate a miracle!" Well, this fantastic mental form does exist. The mind of the young child shows this phenomenon that has remained hidden in the mysteries of the creative unconscious.

If this happens in the case of language—the construction of sounds fashioned by man during centuries of intellectual efforts to chisel the expression of thought —it is easy to acknowledge that in a similar way the other characteristics that differentiate one race from another must be fixed in the child. These are the habits and customs, prejudices and feelings, and generally all those characteristics that we feel to be incarnate within ourselves—features that are part of us independently and even in spite of changes that our intelligence, logic, and reason might wish to bring about. I remember Gandhi once saying, "I could approve of and follow many customs of Western people, but I could never cancel from my soul the worship of the cow." How many may think, "Yes, my religion appears absurd according to logic, but there remains in me, and in spite of me, a mysterious feeling of devotion towards sacred objects—a need to have recourse to them in order to live." Those people who have grown up with the impression of their taboos cannot wipe them out even when they become doctors of philosophy. The child really builds up something. He reproduces in himself, as by a form of psychic mimesis, the characteristics of the people in his environment. Thus while growing up, he does not merely become a *man*—he becomes a *man of his race.*

With this description we have touched a psychic secret of vital importance to humanity; the secret of *adaptation.*

Adaptation

Adaptation, as conceived by the theories of evolution, would end in producing the "characteristics of the species" that differentiate them one from another, until these characteristics are fixed and transmitted unaltered by means of heredity.

Man has to adapt himself to all kinds of conditions and circumstances in the environment and never fixes himself in his habits because he evolves continuously along the course of the history of civilization. He, therefore, must possess a quick acting "power of adaptation," which substitutes for heredity in the psychic field. This power of adaptation, although fully proved by the fact that there are men in all the geographical regions of the earth, at all latitudes, and on all levels, from sea level to that of the highest mountains, does not, however, belong to the adult. The adult does not easily adapt himself once the racial characteristics have been fixed in him. He lives *well* only in that particular area and feels happy only when he is *immersed* in an environment sharing the character features that have been fixed in him.

The adaptation achieved by an adult who emigrates or goes to live among people with different customs is the result of an *effort*, often quite painful. Explorers are heroes; those who live far from the center of their life are exiles.

Once a person has adapted himself, he is happy only in his own center, among the conditions established in his own racial group. The Eskimo feels the fascination of the Arctic environment, just as the Ethiopian is attracted by the jungle. He who has lived by the seacoast is fascinated by the ocean, and the people of the desert enjoy the poetry of the arid and infinite plain. Those who are not *adapted* suffer from the effort to be so. Missionaries consider their lives as a sacrifice.

The child is the instrument who not only makes everyone love his own corner of the earth and attaches him to his own customs, but he is also, and for the same reason, the vehicle that transports mankind through the evolution of civilization. Every man is adapted to his own times and lives well in them. Just as we would be unable to adapt ourselves to the social way of life of a thousand years ago, so a person of that bygone age, when there were no machines or means of rapid communication, would be unable to live among the noise and hurry of our day. He would be terrorized by the miracles man has accomplished by his discoveries, while we find in our environment the pleasure or as we put it, the comforts of life.

The mechanism of this basic adaptation is simple and plain—the child incarnates the environment that he finds around in himself and constructs a man adapted to live in those surroundings. In order to realize this function, the child lives through an initial period of psychoembryonic construction, which is found only in human beings. During this period he lives in a hidden way and is, apparently, an empty and inert being.

Only since the first decade of our century has the child begun to be studied. All those who have studied him have reached the conclusion that the first two years of life are the most important because during that period the fundamental features of development that characterize the human personality are established. While the newly born possesses nothing—not even the power of voluntary movement—the child of two talks, runs, understands, and recognizes things in the environment. His infancy continues further during the period of play when he organizes his unconscious creations and makes them conscious to himself.

Life is divided into well-defined periods. Each

period develops properties, the construction of which is guided by laws of nature.

If these laws are not respected, the construction of the individual may become abnormal, even monstrous. But if we take care of them, are interested in discovering them, and cooperate with them, unknown and surprising character features—which we never even suspected—may result. Gradually we recognize in them the inner mysterious functions that direct the psychic creation of man.

The child possesses great powers that we have not yet been able to utilize.

At the present stage of civilization one of the most imminent perils is that of going *against nature's law* in the education of the child, to suffocate and deform him under the error of common prejudices.

Contact with the World

Meanwhile, a logical conclusion follows: If the child, from birth onwards, has to create his personality at the expense of his environment, he must be brought into contact with the *world*, with the outward life of man. He ought to take part in, or better still, he ought to be in touch with the life of adults. If the child has to incarnate the language of his people he ought to hear them talk and be present at their conversations. If he is to adapt himself to the environment he ought to take part in public life and be a witness of the customs that characterize his race.

What a strange and impressive conclusion! If the child is a recluse in the nursery, withdrawn from social life, he will consequently be repressed, underdeveloped, and deformed. Finally he will become abnormal and *incapable* of adaptation because he has been deprived of the means necessary to accomplish this great function!

Should a small child who can neither speak nor walk be brought into society, to public functions, to take part in the life of adults? Who would dare to make such a suggestion, to attempt such a profound reversal of our modern prejudices.

Even in the face of the evidence that today there is an ever increasing number of problem children, backward children, children who lack in character and initiative, children with a poor command of language who hesitate and stammer and grow up to be unbalanced, adults suffering from psychic abnormality that obstructs their social life—and all this in spite of much hygienic care and almost continual sleep—even in the face of this evidence, many people would reply, "Those things are indeed an evil, but your remedy is absurd!"

Let us then have recourse to nature, because if this creative adaptation is a vital social function of the newly born, nature must have made provision for its protection and facilitation.

Well, we observe that in a natural and primitive form of life there happens exactly what we are advocating. The newly born, the small child, the *spiritual embryo*, who from his environment has to prepare and construct the characteristics proper to his race, always takes part in the social life of the adult. The mother carries the child in her arms and keeps him with her wherever she goes. The peasant woman goes to the fields with her child, brings him to market or to church with her, and he is present while she chats with her neighbors.

Lactation is the tie that still keeps the spiritual embryo attached to its mother. This is a fact common to all races. Even more, the very way in which mothers carry their babies, leaving their hands free for their work, is a characteristic trait of different peoples. The Eskimo mother keeps the child on her back; the Japanese mother ties him to her shoulders; the Indian mother carries him on her hip; while in some cantons in Switzerland, the mother carries her baby on her head. These mothers accomplish a second natural function, of a psychic nature. They unconsciously perform an action necessary for the salvation of the species. Mothers are anything but "revolutionaries in education." They are not teachers of their children. They do not ask them to look about or to learn. They are simply "means of conveyance." They do not at all bother about what the child observes. For them, as for everybody else, the child is an empty being, mute, incapable of intelligent activity or movement. This could almost be called a providential disposition of nature, because what the mother observes is not observed by the child and vice versa.

It is interesting to observe these facts in a primitive crowd, e.g., in a village market where there are people, animals, and all kinds of objects, fruits, cloth, etc., where people discuss their affairs. There we can see how the baby who is still breast-fed, this embryonic infant, looks at many things with a strangely fixed stare. He looks at the *environment* in its various aspects, while the mother stops to do her shopping

and to speak to people. The *world*, the environment in
its totality, escapes the mother's attention but not
that of the infant. The mother looks at the fruits she
wants to buy; the infant is fascinated when he sees
a dog or a donkey moving about. Mother and child
are completely independent in their interests. The child
is actually often carried by or attached in such a way
to his mother that he must necessarily look in the opposite direction. Most of the mother's friends who may
meet her will stop to say something nice to the baby
and unintentionally give him many repeated language
lessons.

In primitive races, lactation is very long—it lasts
more than a year or even two. During all this very
important period of life the child makes the conquest
of the environment. It is really unnecessary for the body
that the child should be fed with its mother's milk
for so long, but the mother follows an instinct of love
by not detaching herself from her child and by carrying
him with her all the time though naturally his weight
increases.

A French missionary, who studied especially the
customs of the Bantu people in central Africa, was
astonished by the fact that the mothers do not even
think of detaching themselves from their children.
They consider them as part of themselves. When attending a solemn royal installation that missionary saw
the queen arrive, child in arms, and she received the
honors of a sovereign while keeping her child with her
all the time. He also marveled that Bantu women can
keep up breast-feeding for so long a period. Generally
it lasts two full years. In other words, it lasts for the

whole epoch that nowadays is of such special interest to modern psychologists.

These natural customs can certainly not be considered revolutionary. We observe them with admiration and attribute to them the merit of the unperturbed character of these children who are not difficult and do not present the "problems" ours do. The secret wholly lies in two words—milk and love.

Nature, wise nature, must be the basis on which a *supranature*, still more perfect, can be constructed. It is certain that progress must *surpass* nature and adopt different forms—it may not, however, proceed by trampling upon nature.

These brief points open a practical path for those generic assertions that begin to invade our scientific world when it is said: "Education must begin at birth."

Conclusions

Man is not a vegetating body that lives on material nourishment only, nor is he destined to sensual emotions alone. Man is that superior being who is endowed with intelligence and is destined to do a great task on earth. He must transform it, conquer it, utilize it, and construct a *new world* full of marvels that surpasses and overrules the wonders of nature. It is man who creates civilization. This work is unlimited, and it is the aim of his physical limbs. From his first appearance on earth, man has been a worker.

The oldest relics of man's achievement are the stones chipped by him according to his needs, which will increase and extend to infinity. He has become the dominator of all living beings, of all substances, and of the very energies scattered throughout the universe. It seems, therefore, "natural to man" that the child should begin by absorbing the environment and accomplish his development by means of work, of gradual experiences in his surroundings. He nourishes and develops his human qualities first by this unconscious absorption and then by his activities directed to outward things. He constructs himself; he forms his characteristics by nourishing his spirit.

If development were limited to physical growth, the child would be condemned to a kind of *hunger* of the mind, which could never be appeased. He would fall victim to the grave evils of "psychic undernourishment." Nothing human could normally develop in him.

Only a few people, so far, have discovered that the evident psychic abnormalities of modern childhood, which reveal themselves from the first years of life, are due to two things—"mental malnutrition" and "a lack of intelligent and spontaneous activity." They are due, in other words, to a repression of vital energies, destined to develop the soul of man. They are caused by a demolition of the laws that guide the growth of the child step by step.

The civilized world becomes an immense concentration camp to which all men are banished and where they are all enslaved, undervalued, and annihilated in their creative impulses, withdrawn from the life-giving stimuli that every man has a right to find among those who love him.

This vague expression could be rendered concrete in the following way: "A new education from birth onward must be built up. Education must be reconstructed and based on the laws of nature and not on the preconceived notions and prejudices of adult men."

Education today is not even based on a scientific approach to man as a whole, because nowadays a treatment of children "from birth" is being evolved that rests only on what hygiene has seen fit to prescribe —good nourishment, especially artificial food. This is facilitated by removing the mother who readily agrees that she has no more milk, isolation of the child in a nursery, and entrusting him to an unknown woman who has no maternal love for him. The child is sentenced to sleep in artificial darkness provided by defending him against daylight. When he is brought out-of-doors, he is trailed along in a covered carriage so that he sees nothing. As he is pushed along he has only the nurse in front of him, and she is a kind of "infirmarian," often quite old, as it is supposed. that older women are more experienced in the care of children. The affectionate looks of a beautiful young mother become something unknown to the child. He is a vegetating body. Medical specialists and psychoanalysts even dare to say that he is a "digestive tube." The silence required to make him sleep takes the place of the human voice. This "digestive tube" is very well studied. The quantity and quality of his rigorously regulated and graded food is measured. The body is regularly weighed to follow up its growth. The caressing movements, which a mother instinctively makes on her child's limbs, are abolished; yet it is nature that inspired them for they are stimuli to life, a call towards consciousness—a delicate massage that prepares the muscles, as yet inert, by means of a passive exercise necessary when the voluntary movements have not yet been developed.

It is truly a strange situation! There is felt a terror lest the caresses of and contact with the mother should be dangerous and indecent, lest they provoke sexual instincts in a being that has barely come into the world. But without these caresses the children may be in danger of losing their character, the power of adaptation and orientation in the complicated world into which they are born.

It is imperative that society should awaken from such deep-rooted errors and deliver these prisoners of misguided civilization. It must prepare for them a *world* adapted to their supreme needs, which are psychic needs.

One of the most urgent endeavors to be undertaken on behalf of the reconstruction of society is the reconstruction of education. It must be brought about by giving the children the environment that is adapted to their life. Well, then, the first environment is the world and the other environments, such as the family and the school, must correspond and satisfy those creative impulses that tend to realize human perfection following the guide of the cosmic laws.

When prejudice will be vanquished by knowledge, then there will appear in the world a "superior child" with his marvelous powers that today remain hidden. Then there will appear the child who is destined to form a humanity capable of understanding and controlling our present civilization.

Part III

World Illiteracy

1

World Illiteracy

THE question of illiteracy presents itself again in our days with new vigor as a problem of great acutality. It is no longer exhausted, as in the past, by compiling cold statistics or by drawing geographical maps showing the percentage of illiterates who, in various proportions, still exist even in the countries of Europe and America.

Since the Second World War, social problems have been studied on a scale that surpasses national and even continental boundaries, areas with a certain uniformity of race and civilization, and that extends to the world as a whole. As a consequence of the war, the Asian peoples—so-called Orientals—have entered the sphere of the social interest of those of the West with a clear consciousness that all the peoples of the world are now closely connected. Some historic events, such as the independence of India and other Asian countries and, at the same time, the efforts to contribute with the help of education to a universal understanding in the interest of all, place the problem of illiteracy among the great pressing questions of the day. That hundreds of millions of illiterates should still exist in the world, while on all continents the products and instruments of mechanized civilization are being spread, reveals the existence of a glaring contrast between the material and the moral progress of man and creates a universal lack of balance. In fact UNESCO, which studies education also as a practical means necessary to establish greater harmony among all peoples, places in the forefront the campaign against illiteracy.

The problem of education certainly is not identical to that of illiteracy—indeed, it is very different. It concerns the spiritual formation and the intellectual uplift of mankind in order to adapt it to the changed conditions in the "new world" where, up till now, it vegetated, unprepared and unconscious. This education, however, must *circulate* by means of literacy, as trains circulate by means of a network of railways.

Thus independent India today places the education of her people among her most urgent tasks.

The problem of providing food for everybody is followed immediately by that of creating schools for all children and cultural institutions for adults. Eastern governments realize that illiteracy is a fundamental question in need of a solution.

A similar problem arose a century and a half ago in the nations of Europe and America. They determined that illiteracy and ignorance should be removed gradually by imparting to all a knowledge of what the English call the "three R's"—Reading, Writing, and Reckoning—but especially Reading and Writing

Great obstacles were immediately thrown in the way of this attempt, because there was no previous experience to indicate the road ahead. Many mistakes were made. Eastern countries can consider themselves fortunate since both obstacles and errors can now be avoided! The experience gathered in the West is of great value to them. The path has been traced and they can advance with rapid steps towards the desired goal.

In Europe the errors caused by inexperience in a rapid and total realization of child education fell back on the children. They became the victims of a kind of slavery without precedent in human history.

Few people know that the first impulse to the realization of this colossal social effort was given by a revolution that initiated a new era in Europe. It marked, in fact, the beginning of the great scientific discoveries and the use of machinery on a vast scale.

The French Revolution of 1789 presented a strange phenomenon. Amidst the savage violence of a popular insurrection, the people themselves claimed that among the rights of man there should be that of the possession of a superior language—the written language. It was a strange, unprecedented claim. It had nothing to do with the reaction against an oppressive power that impoverished the people. The people, therefore, did not only ask for bread and work, as they did later, following the teaching of Marx—nor did they limit their claims to a change in the social hierarchies and political government. They revindicated the human right to be instructed in order to be in a position to avail themselves of Article XI of the Declaration of the Rights of Man and Citizen sanctioned in 1791. The article reads: "The free communication of thoughts and opinions is one of the most precious of the rights of Man. Every citizen, therefore, may speak, write, print freely." It was certainly one of the few instances of people asking to be given an opportunity to make a new acquisition instead of asking for a decrease of work, because the acquisition thus claimed had to be made by the effort of each individual for himself at the cost of painful labor.

This request was born of something considerably greater than the desire to break the chains of tyranny. In fact, three years were needed to establish the principles of a new social life and to overthrow the monarchy, but a century was needed to extend to all a knowledge of the written language.

Although the war cry was "liberty," the conquest of literacy was not made through liberty because compulsion was found to be necessary. The practical fulfilment of the colossal task was not accomplished by the destruction of a monarchy that had exploited the people. It was actually the conquest of another monarchy, that of the first French Empire. Napoleon, the paladin of the French Revolution, gave new strength to the people and, by preventing the reestablishment of old conditions, led the people decisively to a new life. Under his magic touch, the French masses became as a tidal wave breaking through the boundaries of centuries. His epic feats led to the only true conquest—which remains to the present day—the uplift of the people to an intellectual level according to the rights of man.

With the Code of Napoleon, compulsory education made its first appearance in the legislation of the nations. And because Napoleon imposed his code on the peoples of Europe, this principle of education conquered not only France but the whole empire on the morrow of the terrible destructions of the war.

Compulsory education was established in many European states; then it passed to America. Thus the slow and difficult task of eliminating illiteracy was started. All the civilized nations of those days took it up.

The education of the masses opened a new chapter in human history, and it continued to be developed and expanded. It proclaimed a task requiring a mental effort from every individual, and the task was entrusted to the children.

In the first years of the nineteenth century the child entered history as an active factor in the progress of civilization. At the same time, however, he became a victim. The child could not understand, as did the adult, the necessity of this conquest essential to social life. Mobilized from the age of six years, childhood only felt the sufferings of imprisonment and the slavery of being compelled to learn the alphabet and the art of writing. This was a dry and boring task, the importance and future advantages of which he could not appreciate. Banished to heavy desks, urged on by punishments, he had to learn under coercion and to sacrifice not only his weak body but also his personality.

Thus it has always been in the painful history of men. All the great conquests have been made at the cost of slavery. The great Egyptian monuments, the expansion of Rome across the seas, all required as a first necessity the sacrifice of men, forced with the whip to perform the hard and monotonous labor of transporting blocks of stone or rowing the galleys. And also for this new conquest of a higher degree of intelligence in order to acquire the universal use of reading and writing, mankind needed slaves; these slaves were the children.

At the beginning of the twentieth century a movement was started to improve the conditions under which children passed their sentence of "hard labor." However much has been achieved in this line, the child is nevertheless even today far from being given the consideration that his *natural human rights* demand.

It is not yet sufficiently realized that the child who studies at school is a *potential* "man," that his value does not consist merely in serving as an instrument by means of which people will rise to a higher level of culture, reach national aims, and obtain practical advantages for society. The child possesses "values of his own." If humanity must be improved, the child has to be understood better; he must be respected and helped. Humanity, in fact, will remain as imperfect as it is today if different levels of development and the consequent lack of harmony, which prevents it from advancing on the road of progress, persist. The succession of unfortunate events in our days proves it; it becomes, therefore, urgent and essential to cultivate the human energies in themselves.

In the countries where compulsory education is making its first appearance today, the experience of the past can be put to precious account and the start can be made from a higher level. The child must no longer be considered as a means of progress, as a slave on whose shoulders the burden of the progress of civilization can be dumped. Education must begin with a view to helping the development of the child himself and thereby as an increment to the potentialities of the people.

The needs of the child, the help necessary for his life, must be the fundamental concern of modern education.

"The needs of the child" are more than simply those of his physical life. Those of his intelligence and personality as a human being are equally urgent and much loftier. Ignorance is even more fatal to man than is undernourishment or poverty.

Many people think that respect for the child and consideration for his psychical life means to leave the child alone, in inertia, i.e., without any mental activity. On the contrary, when the natural energies are taken as the basis, or in other words, when the plan of education follows the special psychology of the development of man, not only rapid and extensive progress is made but also an intensification of personal values is realized.

The progress of our civilization rests on a scientific basis, and consequently education too must be planned on this same basis.

To learn to read and to write is the beginning of compulsory education, the foundation on which it is based; and so reading and writing are considered the first subjects to be taught. However, it is necessary to distinguish them from the rest of culture. Possession of the art of writing is not a mere skill; it represents the possession of a superior form of language added to its natural form. Written language complements spoken language and is integrated with it. Spoken language is developed naturally in every man. Without it he would be miserable, cut off from society, a deaf-and-dumb creature. Language is one of the characteristics that distinguish man from the animals. It is a gift of nature bestowed on him alone. It is an expression of his intelligence.

What would be the purpose of such an intelligence if man were not able to understand and transmit his thoughts? Without language how would he associate with other men to achieve a common enterprise, to perform work?

Spoken language is like a breath of air that can reach only the ear that happens to be close to it. That is why men, from remotest antiquity onward, have looked for means to transmit their thoughts over a great distance and to fix their remembrance. Graphic signs were chiselled upon rocks or written on the skins of animals. From these attempts, through many transformations, the alphabet gradually evolved. This was an acquisition of paramount importance! "This conquest," writes Diringer, in *The Alphabet* (Hutchinson's, London and New York, 1949), "is greater and of more importance than all others for the progress of civilization because it enables us to unite the thoughts of the whole of mankind all along the successive development of the generations. The alphabet concerns not only this out-ward development, but the very nature of man, because it completes the natural language by adding another form of expression to it."

If man is superior to the animals, which have no articulate language, then the man who can read and write is superior to one who can only speak; and it is the man who writes who alone possesses the language necessary to the culture of our times. Written language, therefore, must not be considered merely as a subject in schools, and a part of culture. It is, rather, a *characteristic of civilized man.*

The civilization of our days cannot make progress among people who possess only spoken language, and illiteracy becomes, therefore, the greatest obstacle to progress.

By chance I learned recently the following bit of news. In China, besides the movements of Chiang Kai-shek and the Communists, there is a third movement started by a young man who has dedicated his intelligence to the simplification of the Chinese script. He meets a need of his country that no one before him had fully understood. The traditional Chinese script that is in use requires the knowledge of at least 9,000 characters. This makes it impossible to remove the ignorance of the masses. That young reformer, without introducing new ideas, new forms of government, or better economic conditions, or even freedom, has nevertheless acquired great popularity in China.

He is evidently a great benefactor of the Chinese

people, who feel the need of taking part in world progress—a progress only to be reached with the uplift of the human personality. The Chinese people feel that their first and fundamental right is that of possessing the two languages necessary for civilized man. The two languages are the starting point. Culture will come later.

It is, therefore, necessary to realize these points in the schools: on the one hand, the two languages connected with the formation of man; on the other, culture to be acquired at a second stage.

In view of this, I shall outline the experience gathered from the study of children, as this can be of great advantage to those who are striving to eliminate illiteracy. *Written language can be acquired much more easily by children of four years than by those of six years of age—the time at which compulsory education usually starts.* While children of six years of age need at least two years to learn how to write and do so with much difficulty and against nature, children of four years learn this second language within a few months.

Not only do they acquire it without pain or effort, but with great enthusiasm. A phenomenon that, more than forty years ago, kindled in me the desire to dedicate my life to education was the spontaneous phenomenon of the "explosion of writing" in children of four years of age.

This fact, which I shall try to illustrate below, has an immense importance of practical value. If, indeed, so-called compulsory education begins with illiterate children of six years of age, they meet with great difficulties because at that period of life it means a waste of time and energy to learn writing and reading, and it imposes upon children an arid mental effort that breeds a certain disgust towards study and all intellectual instruction.

It takes away the appetite for knowledge before one has even begun to nourish oneself with it. When, instead, children of six years of age would already know how to read and write, the school could immediately begin by imparting culture in an easy and interesting way, and the children would enter the field of study with enthusiasm.

The difference is fundamental. Really rational and modern schools capable of obtaining an uplift from the people must be able to count upon these *new children*— on those who already possess the two languages and on the children of the superior man who is adapted to live in our times.

All schools begin always by teaching reading and writing because written matter fixes human knowledge. It is, therefore, a logical procedure; as the aim of the school is to impart knowledge, it is necessary that children be given the means to make this knowledge durable. Reading and writing are the keys that can disclose the immense reserves of human knowledge, collected, fixed, and accumulated in books by means of the art of writing. Yet, as I said before, the two things must be distinguished—writing, which is an art in itself, and knowledge.

Writing has become accessible to all since the invention of the alphabet, which has simplified it so that it is within the reach even of children.

That invention has not merely simplified, but also

humanized writing because it has connected written language directly with spoken language and made the former a complement of the latter.

Spoken language is made up of but few sounds because these depend upon the possibilities of continuing the movements of the vocal organs that have their own limitations. These limitations are the same for the whole of mankind. In some languages only twenty-four or twenty-six essential sounds are used; in others more, but the sounds are always limited. On the other hand, the combinations of these sounds, i.e., the number of words, is unlimited or practically so. A language can be enriched in words without limit. No dictionary contains them all. No dictionary can contain the words one could make by combining letters and syllables according to the mathematical laws of permutations and combinations.

The alphabetically written language consists in giving a representation by means of a graphic sign to each sound composing a word. The result is that these signs are few in number, as few as the basic sounds. This representation has been perfectly achieved in the so-called phonetic languages. Nevertheless, each alphabetically written language is more or less perfectly based on this simple principle. The fact that not all alphabetic scripts correspond phonetically to the spoken language is a difficulty caused by the incomplete application of the alphabet according to its meaning. This difficulty, however, could be corrected, and writing would become correspondingly easier. There is, in fact, no doubt that languages and their translations in writing are still in the course of evolution. They are still on the road to perfection.

This is the reason why the learning of writing ought to begin with an analysis of the sounds of the words. That is the path to be followed.

Writing should not begin with those books, used even today in ordinary schools, that start by giving syllables and printed words—the primers.

The correct use of the alphabet in learning to write should only give the simple signs of the alphabet itself in order to put them in direct relation with the sounds they represent.

Then the combinations of the written words could derive directly from the spoken language that already exists in its entirety in the mind. This procedure is so simple that it can lead to writing as if by magic. The signs of the alphabet, in fact, are generally so simple and easily shaped and they are so few that all can remember them.

Logical reasoning leads to the conclusion that if this procedure were applied, writing would come spontaneously and would immediately represent the whole spoken language that each one possesses.

With this key the problem of learning to write would be solved without any trouble. It would be possible not only to learn to write in a few months, but writing would also *develop spontaneously* and become gradually more complete as the mind concentrated on this exercise.

The alphabet in direct connection with spoken language—that is the way to achieve the art of writing by following an *inner path*. The ability to write will be acquired as a result of the analysis of the words each one possesses and of the activity of one's own mind, which is interested in such a magical conquest.

If, instead, writing is made to start from books, hence from the capacity to read—and if such books give groups of arbitrarily chosen words that have to be learned—then the difficulties are increased. The result will be a separate language—a written language taken from without and derived from the deciphering of syllables or words without any interest.

It is as if an attempt were made to construct from without another language beginning with senseless, babbling sounds as happens in early infancy during the first year of life. The procedure followed would be similar to that used by nature when articulate speech is built up in a being without intelligence and voluntary movement, as is man at birth.

If, instead, the alphabet is linked up with spoken language, the process becomes that of simply translating one's own language in graphic signs.

Then it is always connected with words that have a meaning for the mind, and the progress of writing takes place by a natural attraction. The language possessed then becomes twofold and persists by being fixed in a stable form. The eyes and the hand act together upon the treasure naturally accumulated by means of hearing and of the vocal organs. Yet, while spoken language is a breath that disappears into space, written language becomes a permanent object that remains fixed in front of the eye and can be manipulated and studied.

It is on account of its direct relation to the sounds of words that the alphabet represents one of the greatest inventions of mankind.

The alphabet has influenced human progress more than any other invention because it has modified man himself, furnishing him with new powers above those of nature. It has made man the possessor of two languages—a natural and a supranatural one. With the latter, man can transmit his thoughts to faraway people. He can fix them for his descendants. He can practically build up a treasure of the intellectual products of the whole of humanity through time and space.

"It is surprising," writes Diringer, "that the history of writing should be a Cinderella, as much to the educated as to the uneducated. This history is not a subject of study at the University, nor in Secondary Schools, nor in primary schools and no important museum has ever considered it necessary to offer to the public a demonstrative exhibition on the development of writing." (D. Diringer: *The Alphabet*)[1]

Concentrated on outer progress, man has not given sufficient attention to this magical instrument.

Writing is not identical to the alphabet. Writing consists of a series of attempts to transmit thought in a practical and permanent way. Its history goes back thousands of years. At first man tried to represent the objects of his thoughts by means of drawings; then he tried to symbolize ideas by signs; and only much later did he find a simple solution in the alphabet.

It is not the ideas that have to be represented by pictures but the language in its component sounds, because only language can genuinely represent ideas and the contents of more elaborate thought. The alphabet permits us to do this because it translates the spoken word faithfully.

---

[1]Diringer has since established such a museum at Cambridge, England— Trans.

The function of the alphabet has not been taken into consideration in the ordinary method of teaching writing. It is presented only as an analysis of the written language, instead of what in fact it is—the faithful reproduction of the spoken language. It has remained submerged in writing and its own purpose has not been stressed, nor does it arouse any interest.

It is, therefore, an arid beginning of a study, the purpose and advantage of which remain hidden from the mind of the child for a long time. The written language, even in perfectly phonetic languages, is taught in just the same way as would be taught Chinese script, in which there is no relation between the signs and the sounds composing a word, which does not therefore possess the marvelous and practical simplicity of the alphabet.

Our experiment, begun in Rome in 1907 with children between three and six years of age, was, I believe, the first and only example of an attempt to teach writing by directly connecting the graphic signs of the alphabet with the spoken language without the use of books. The marvelous and unexpected result was that writing came "as an explosion" and began at once with whole words that flowed incessantly from the mind of the child. By means of their little hands they covered blackboards, floors, and walls with written words in an indefatigable and exalting creative activity. This astounding phenomenon occurred among children of four to four and a half years of age.

I am sure that this old experience will prove useful today in the fight against illiteracy, as it enables us to use the resources of nature.

To put writing in its real and simple aspects, i.e., to connect it directly with the spoken language, is already in itself a practical step forward and this can be applied to children as well as to adults. Writing thus becomes a form of self-expression and awakens an interest and activity, exalted by the enthusiasm engendered by an evident conquest and the acquisition of a new power.

After the first phase, which establishes writing in the individual, it becomes a talisman enabling its holder to penetrate into the ocean of culture and opens up to him, more or less widely, a new world. Books, readers and primers, must, therefore, be abolished during this first period when writing is being acquired as a new form of self-expression. The alphabet then represents a key that is turned from within.

Culture proper is distinct from writing. Yet, if an illiterate man of wide experience and moral value can be imagined as existing before the invention of the alphabet, in our days it is inconceivable that such an illiterate person, whatever be his moral greatness, should take a real part in the culture characteristic of his time.

The two different aspects that can be distinguished when considering language can be of great practical help.

The written language concerns self-expression. It is a very simple mechanism to be introduced into the personality. It can be analyzed in its parts, and precisely this analysis is of the greatest value.

To be a man of letters or not, i.e., ignorant in the cultural sense, is not the same thing as knowing how to write or not.

Writing stands in relation to the alphabet only and

consequently with spoken speech and an analysis of its sounds. To be a man of letters, educated and cultured, means to have penetrated literature that is linked up with the outer world—with books fixing images and thoughts, in other words, with reading.

Our experiences with children of four years of age (when writing can "explode" as a result of a conquest already made) were especially important. The fundamental development of language continues in fact up to the age of five years, and the mind during this period is in a phase of activity regarding everything that has to do with words.

This is the time—we might call it the "season in life"—when written language can ripen as does a fruit. The ripening of fruit does not depend solely on the kind of seed sown and the preparation of the soil, but very much also on the season when it was sown.

The analysis of writing, which in its mechanism permits us to link it up with spoken language by means of the alphabet, can be useful to adults as well as to children, but the favorable season is when spoken language is in course of completing and perfecting itself spontaneously. This is the "sensitive psychic period" placed by nature in the child for this purpose. We can here really use the term "development of written language" because by placing the alphabet in contact with the sounds of the words the two languages develop, expand, and are enriched as if they formed one organic whole.

The preparation of the mechanism is a natural process. Spoken language begins by prolonged babbling, which makes the organs of speech function mechanically. Only at two years of age, when these movements are established, does language develop more directly under the urge of the intelligence, which absorbs new words and continues to perfect the actual construction of language, absorbing it from the environment and the people among whom the child lives. There are then two different phases—one in which the mechanism (i.e., the smooth functioning of the organs of speech) is prepared by means of long exercises; and the other, an intellectual phase in which language is developed in its expressive construction.

In this second phase the alphabet can be of help to its further growth in perfection in the same way as the intelligence in the adult is perfected by the acquisition of culture, when he knows how to read and write.

The important fact is that the alphabet and the subsequent ability to write *help* the development of language in the child. As it is of real help to the natural development that takes place at this period, it is absorbed with vital eagerness.

The signs of the alphabet, as we give them, embodied in separate objects that can be handled, act not only as stimuli drawing the activity of the consciousness towards the articulate language that had first been acquired unconsciously and leading to an analysis of the sounds composing the words, but they also give to these sounds a visible shape that remains all the time before the eye.

The *moveable alphabet*[2] is a docile instrument that

---

[2]The *moveable alphabet* is part of the *means of development* offered by the Montessori Method. *See* Maria Montessori: *The Discovery of the Child.*—Trans.

the hand can move about making different combinations and constructing different words as one does with the various pieces of a puzzle. It thus guides the child to make a marvelous conquest.

What conquest could be more marvelous indeed?

Those few objects enable the child to construct *all the words* that he possesses, even those spoken by others. This simple intellectual exercise represents, therefore, a help to determine, perfect, and consolidate the spoken language.

The basis of these exercises is evidently the analysis of words, i.e., spelling according to the sounds (not according to the artificial names of the letters). It is a completely inner exercise that permits the child to pass in review his own language in its component parts. This the child had never done before, nor could he ever do it without the key furnished by these visible and moveable signs.

The child thus *discovers* his own language. Each attempt to construct a word is based upon an investigation and a discovery, the discovery of the sounds forming the word he wishes to reproduce.

These exercises can be of interest also to the illiterate adult, and it has been proved in fact that they do interest him.[3] The alphabet can be for everybody a key that leads to the exploration of one's language and arouses a new interest. Interest is awakened not merely on account of this analysis, which helps to overcome

---

[3]The Italian "National Union for the Struggle against Illiteracy" asked Dr. Montessori to write a pamphlet, which was published in Rome in 1951 with the title *Introduzione ad un Metodo per Insegnare a Leggere e a Scrivere agli Adulti (Introduction to a Method to Teach Writing and Reading to Adults)*, and which has since been applied with much success.—Trans.

the difficulties of correct spelling in the written language, but also because it makes us aware of the fact that the letters of the alphabet are so few in number. Yet few though they be, they can express the whole language in every form and on every occasion. If, for example, an adult knows a poem or a prayer by heart, all the words of that poem or prayer can be constructed. It is bewildering to reflect that all the books of a whole library, all the news that daily fills the pages of innumerable newspapers, are all combinations of the alphabetic signs. The conversations heard in one's environment, the speeches transmitted by the radio are all composed of those very same sounds represented by these few objects—the letters of the alphabet! It is easy to imagine that someone who is illiterate may find himself uplifted in spirit on becoming conscious of this. It may well be a revelation and inspiration to him.

It is not these ideas, however, that fascinate the child, but in him vital energies are at work. Exercises with the alphabet give him exalting emotions because during the period of development of language there is in him a living flame that burns in an effort at creation.

In our first schools the children often held up cardboard pieces showing the letters of the alphabet, waving them in the air as if they were banners and revealing the impetus of their enthusiasm by their jubilant cries.

In my books I have mentioned children who walked about by themselves, like monks in meditation, softly analyzing words—saying to themselves "to make Sofia you need s-o-f-i-a" (mentioning the individual sounds not names of the letters).

Once a father asked his child who attended our school, "Have you been good today?" to which the child replied with emphasis, "Good—g–oo–d."

What had struck him was the word; and immediately he analyzed it into its component sounds.

The exercises with the moveable alphabet place the whole language in motion. They provoke a real intellectual activity.

It should be noted, however, that in all these exercises the hand does *not write*. The child can build long and difficult words without ever having written, without ever having held a pen in his hand.

The exercise of composing words is only a *preparation* for writing. Yet in this exercise both reading and writing are potentially included—writing because the exercise results objectively in written words, and reading because when one looks at these words and interprets them, one reads. These continuous exercises, therefore, by means of which both spoken and written words are built up, do not only prepare the way for writing but for *correct* spelling as well.

In ordinary schools words are usually incorrectly spelled when children start to write. This serious difficulty encountered in ordinary schools (in the United States there are even clinics for orthography now) is entirely solved by the word-building exercises with the moveable alphabet. They prepare the way for reading without books, and the way for writing without actually writing.

It is, as I defined it, "written language delivered from its mechanisms."

Real writing, i.e., with the hand tracing the letters of the alphabet with a pen, is only an executory mechanism. It is so thoroughly detached from the intellectual effort involved in writing that written language can be produced by the typewriter and printing press. The hand is a kind of living machine, the movements of which have to be prepared so that they may render service to the intelligence. This preparation is given by separate exercises that firmly establish the necessary motor coordinations.

The intelligence and the executive organ—here we have another distinction requiring different preparatory processes in practice.

If learning to write is started *while writing*, difficulties are encountered, which although not insuperable, are nevertheless without any doubt a *hindrance* to the mental effort involved. It is as if a person sufficiently intelligent and full of ideas, clamoring to be expressed in speech, did not yet find at his disposal the mechanisms of articulate language. A procedure similar to that followed for writing in ordinary schools is used when an attempt is made to teach deaf and dumb people to speak. This attempt is merely to provoke the movements of articulation by the effort to speak, and it is similar to insisting on the preparation of the hand for writing while trying to make it write.

If a laborer, with his already stiffened hand, starts learning to write with a delicately pointed pen or pencil, he must perform exercises that are very difficult, disagreeable, and discouraging for him. The nib splits, the ink blots, the pencil breaks, and altogether the training is most depressing. The imperfect results he produces put his goodwill to a heroic test.

In primary schools the pen really becomes an

instrument of torture for the children, and writing a form of hard labor imposed by compulsion and continuous punishments.

The hand, too, therefore needs its own preparation. What is needed before one actually writes is to learn writing by means of a series of interesting exercises that form a kind of gymnastics similar to those used to give agility to the muscles of the body.

The hands are external organs, the movements of which can be influenced directly by education. They are in fact visible and simple. They do not, as is the case with the mechanisms of the spoken word, require secret and imperceptible movements of hidden organs like the tongue and the vocal chords.

The hand that writes needs certain coordinations that can be analyzed. They are the holding of the writing instrument between the fingers, the flowing movement necessary to trace with the pen, the meticulous and minute drawing of the letters of the alphabet, while all the time the hand has to be kept light and sure.

These different movements can be prepared one by one by means of different exercises.

As is done for the children in our schools and for adults too, different types of manual work can be thought out, each of which prepares one of these elements.

While moving the objects used in our sensorial exercises, the children's hands are being prepared for all the actions necessary for writing (i.e., the method of indirect preparation for writing in *The Discovery of the Child*, by Dr. Maria Montessori).

It is then necessary only to give an exact indication regarding the manipulation of the writing instruments.

The *exactness* in handling them gives the children a new interest. In the epoch of early childhood, children are urged by nature itself to coordinate the movements of the hands, as is seen by their urge to touch everything, to take everything in their hands, and to play with everything. The hand of the child in the "play age" is led by life itself to lend itself to this indirect preparation for writing. In that epoch also the child has a real passion for drawing. The immense advantage of having a *"new"* hand, animated by natural energies is no longer found either in the adult or even in the child of six years.

He has then already emerged from the sensitive period for these activities (the play age, the age for touching everything). He has, therefore, already established haphazardly the movements of his hands.

The condition of a laborer is still worse, because when he learns to write he must first destroy something that the habit of labor has already fixed in his hand.

Yet precisely in view of this difficulty, it is well to prepare the hand of the illiterate adult indirectly also by some manual exercises and especially by drawing exercises. The drawing should not be free, but executed with precision by the help of some means that guide the hand and permit him to obtain the visible result of well-executed decorative designs.

Thus there would be a kind of gymnastics to prepare the mechanisms of the hand. This preparation can be compared, in view of its goal, to the other intellectual preparation for writing, achieved by means of the moveable alphabet. The mind and the hand are prepared separately for the conquest of written language and follow different roads to the same goal.

The final act, viz., that of tracing effectively with the hand the alphabetic signs that the eye already knows, is now the only thing lacking.

The ordinary methods in use in schools consist of making the child copy letters already traced and held up before his eyes as a model. It seems logical but actually it is purposeless since the movements of the hand have no direct connection with the eyes. *To see* does not sufficiently help the hand *to write*.

The will only is active when it tries to execute writing while looking at a model.

It is different in the case of spoken language, where hearing and the movements of articulation correspond in that mysterious and intimate relationship that is precisely one of the distinctive characteristics of the human species. In the case of writing, to copy is an artificial effort that produces a series of imperfect, wearying, and discouraging attempts.

Now the hand can be prepared directly to trace the signs of the alphabet by the help of the tactile and muscular senses, not by that of sight. We have, therefore, prepared for our children letters cut out in sandpaper and pasted on smooth cardboard. They reproduce in dimension and shape the letters of the moveable alphabet. We teach the children to trace them in the same direction as is followed in writing.

This is a very simple procedure that leads to marvelous results.

Thus the children stamp, so to speak, the shape of the letters on their hands. When they begin to write, spontaneously their penmanship is nearly perfect, and all children write in the same way because all have touched the same letters.

In the case of illiterate laborers the same procedure can be adopted. Any laborer is capable of tracing sandpaper letters, guided by the tactile sensitivity of his fingers. He can thus follow all the particular features of the simple designs corresponding to the letters of the alphabet.

I know that two centuries ago an artist working in the Vatican prepared adults in that way to execute penmanship. In those days books were still written by hand on exquisite parchment scrolls, which were works of art. Beautiful penmanship was a necessary accomplishment of specialists, but even then it was extremely difficult to execute the minute details of perfect writing.

That artist thought of having the models traced by his students instead of copied. He thus succeeded in training calligraphers with a rapidity and preciseness that otherwise would have required a very long period of training, and even then might not have always been successful.

It is as simple as the egg of Columbus—it is practical and logical.

And now, when everything is ready, the hand can write effectively. If the mind has already gone through the exercises on word building, then writing can "explode" all of a sudden; and immediately complete words, even whole sentences, are written as if by magic, as by a new gift of nature.

That is what happens during the famous "explo-

sion into writing" experienced in children of four years
of age. They wrote by reproducing the shapes they
touched and therefore they wrote well. They also wrote
with correct spelling, which was acquired independently by the intelligence in a previous phase.

The rapidity with which the children learn to write
is astounding. In my first experiments, they came into
contact with the alphabet for the first time in the month
of October and already around Christmas they wrote
letters to their benefactors. Earlier even, they already
had written their greetings to visitors on the blackboard.

It is well to remember that their hands had been
prepared indirectly by long handling of the sensorial
apparatus and, also, that the Italian language is almost
perfectly phonetic and can be written entirely with
only twenty-one alphabetic signs.[4]

But even with nonphonetic languages the same
phenomenon occurs, although it takes a bit longer. In
all countries with nonphonetic languages such as
English, Dutch, and German, children six years old were
able to read and write.

Regarding reading, it is already in a sense implied
in the exercises with the moveable alphabet. In a perfectly phonetic language it could be developed without
any further aid if there were a strong impulse to
know the secrets of written matter.

Our small children, on their Sunday walks with
their parents, would stop for a long time in front of

---

[4]The method has also been worked out successfully for Indian languages
and scripts and is explained in the Indian Montessori Training Courses
held under the auspices of the Association Montessori Internationale.

Its practical application can be observed in India, in the A. M. I.
Montessori Houses of Children.—Trans.

the shops and succeed in deciphering the names written outside, although they were in printed capital letters, while they had learned only the letters of the moveable alphabet in cursive script.

They, therefore, accomplished a real work of interpretation similar to that done when the inscriptions of ancient peoples are deciphered.

Such an effort could be evoked only by an intense interest in understanding what was written by deciphering it.

Once, in our first school attended by children whose parents were all illiterate and who, therefore, had no books at home, one of the children brought a piece of crumpled dirty paper saying: "Guess what this is!" "A piece of dirty paper," was the reply. "No—a story!" The other children gathered around him with the greatest astonishment, and all were persuaded of the prodigious truth.

Afterwards they looked for books and would tear out the pages to take them home.

This experience shows that learning to read depends more upon mental activity than upon teaching.

At five years of age the children read whole books, and reading affords them as much satisfaction and entertainment as did the fairy tales and news that adults used to tell them for their amusement.

Children are interested in books when they know how to read. This is so obvious that it seems superfluous to say so.

In ordinary schools, however, reading begins directly with books. There children must learn to read by reading.

The first readers are prepared on the basis of old prejudices, which consider imaginary difficulties to be overcome successively.

At the beginning, short words are given, then longer ones. First simple, then complex syllables, and so on are presented. In other words, obstacles are placed in front of the child at every step.

But these difficulties do not actually exist. The children already know short and long words and all kinds of syllables in their mother tongue. All that is necessary is to analyze the sounds and find the corresponding alphabetic sign for each. That is all—although it may seem difficult for one who is unfamiliar with this truth to understand it! Reading should not be used to overcome difficulties such as those mentioned here.

Reading is the entrance of written language to the field of culture. It is not, like writing, a means of self-expression. It has, instead, for its aim to gather and reconstruct, by means of the alphabetic signs, words and ideas expressed by others who "talk to us in silence."

Reading, too, requires the help of a preparation.

Although it is not possible here to describe in detail the means used by us for this preparation, I will confine myself by repeating that reading does not begin with books. We start it with a series of apparatus consisting of small slips on which are written the names of familiar objects. The child has to recognize the meaning of the word he reads and then place the slip beside the object it indicates. In a second phase we give short sentences indicating actions to be performed. To give "names" teaches the distinction of a particular part of speech—the noun; to give actions makes them distinguish another part of speech—the verb. Thus, the first reading exercises can be prepared in such a way as to introduce the grammatical study of language.[5]

The child of two years of age possesses not only words but their successive combinations necessary to the expression of thought. Words alone do not suffice to convey meaning. A particular order in which they have to be placed is equally necessary.

Each language has its own special order, and this order is transmitted in its entirety by nature to each individual during the first two years of life.

Just as the analysis of words into their component sounds, performed during the period of alphabetic word building, helps the child to realize his own language consciously, in the same way, reading, based on the parts of speech, helps him to acquire consciousness of the grammatical construction and of the functions of each part of speech and the place it should occupy in the sentence.

Grammar thus assumes a kind of "constructive" function on the lines of an analysis, and is not, as is thought in ordinary methods, a kind of anatomy—a dismembering of speech into its parts in order to analyze it.

The small grammatical reading slips are brief, easy, and clear, and at the same time interesting, especially as they are also accompanied by motor activities, not of the hand only but of the whole body.

---

[5]For details cf. *"The Discovery of the Child,"* by Dr. Maria Montessori, Chapters XVII and XVIII.

These active grammatical reading exercises lead to a development of actions and games that help in the exploration of language, i.e., of those modes of self-expression already acquired unconsciously.

The exploration of the language that has already been acquired when the child faces it consciously is thus carried out by means of attractive, practical exercises linked up with reading.

As reading is done with the eyes, the sentences are written in rather large script and with various bright colors to render them more attractive, the different parts of speech also being written in different colors. This not only facilitates reading but makes the distinction between the different parts of speech clear.

At this stage, in this period of life, the child can be helped to correct grammatical defects in his speech, just as at a slightly earlier period the exercises of word building with the moveable alphabet helped his spelling.

In the course of our experience, facts have been revealed, which those who have not penetrated our work and method find it difficult to understand, for instance the fact that there is no successive progression in these exercises. They all go parallel, and those already done are taken up again several times. Those that in ordinary schools would be considered more difficult may precede other exercises that there would be considered easier. All may be done in turn on one and the same morning. It may happen that a five-year-old child who now reads whole books may return to and enthusiastically take part in those grammatical reading exercises and the games connected with them.

Reading, therefore, penetrates directly the level

of culture, because these exercises are not limited to reading only, but form part of a progress in knowledge —the study of one's own language. During this brilliant process of development all grammatical difficulties are met and overcome. Even those minute variations applied to words when they have to be adapted to the details of expressive speech, such as prefixes, suffixes, declensions, etc., become interesting objects of exploration. The conjugation of verbs evokes a kind of philosophical analysis that helps towards understanding that the verb in a sentence represents *the voice that speaks of action*. It is not the indication of an effective action in course of being performed by the speaker. Such reflective exploration of the verb also awakens in the consciousness a notion of the different latitudes of time. The irregular verbs, otherwise so difficult to learn, exist already in the language spoken by the child, and it is now only a question of "discovering" that they are irregular.

All this is different when one has to study a foreign language where everything has to be learned newly.

But is the grammar of one's mother tongue not also studied in ordinary schools?

There the mother tongue is actually studied as if it were a foreign language!

The divine and mysterious work of creation, the greatest miracle of nature is ignored and passed over.

It is easy to understand that these grammatical reading exercises in all their simplicity and clarity can be used also for illiterate adults.

Otherwise in order to learn to read they would have to make the effort of understanding what is written in books, which have no attraction whatever in the monotonous uniformity of their printed type. They require the knowledge of two different alphabets at the same time—the written and the printed scripts—and that is an additional difficulty.

The grammatical exploration of language helps not only reading, but also provides stimulating satisfaction because it renders conscious the language one already possesses. To read books, on the other hand, compels us to concentrate on thoughts coming from without.

Besides, in practice it is not easy to find many teachers who are willing to teach a mass of illiterate adults and who themselves possess a thorough knowledge of grammar. Material that is prepared and ready for use can make up for the imperfections of improvised teachers, while rendering teaching easier for the teachers themselves.

In relation to an experiment recently made in Great Britain after the Second World War, a Scottish teacher said, "I was embarrassed with all the things I had to do, but the apparatus made up for my insufficiency. The class has become a real grammar factory in which all the laborers are busy and cheerful."

Culture in itself, as I said earlier, must not be confused with learning to read and write.

The five-year-old child is cultured not because he possesses written language, but because he is intelligent and will have learned many things.

In fact, our children at six years of age already possess much and varied knowledge in biology, geography, mathematics, etc., which they gain from direct contact with a visible apparatus that can be manipulated.

But that is a subject different from what I wished to deal with here. I intended to deal only with a subject of such great immediacy as the elimination of illiteracy among the masses.

Culture can be transmitted by means of the spoken word, also by the radio and phonographic records. It can be given by the help of projections and films. Above all, however, it has *to be taken in through activity* with the help of an apparatus that permits the child to acquire culture by himself, urged onwards by the nature of his mind that seeks and is guided by the laws of his development. These laws prove that culture is absorbed by the child by means of individual experience, by the repetition of interesting exercises that always require the contribution of the activity of the hand, the organ that cooperates with the development of the intelligence.